W9-CIR-924

From Old Woman to Older Women

From Old Woman to Older Women

Contemporary Culture and Women's Narratives

Sally Chivers

The Ohio State University Press

Columbus

Library of Congress Cataloging-in-Publication Data

Chivers, Sally.
From old woman to older women : contemporary culture and women's
narratives / Sally Chivers.
p. cm.
Includes bibliographical references and index.
ISBN 0-8142-0935-1 (hardcover : alk. paper)
1. Canadian fiction—Women authors—History and criticism. 2. Women and literature—Canada—History—20th century. 3. Canadian fiction—20th century—History and criticism. 4. Aged women in literature. 5. Old age in literature. I. Title.
PR9188 .C47 2003
813'.5093520565—dc21
2003005499

Cover design by Dan O'Dair.
Printed by Thomson-Shore, Inc.

The paper used in this publication meets the minimum requirements of the American National Standard for Information Sciences—Permanence of Paper for Printed Library Materials. ANSI Z39.48-1992.

9 8 7 6 5 4 3 2 1

For Edith Grace Chivers,
who lives to prove the words I write,
and for Margaret Campbell-Ferguson,
whose early death speaks to old age
as a benefit not shared by all.

Contents

Preface

Old Age, Literature, and Potential

At the age of seventeen, completely by chance, I chose Margaret Laurence's *Stone Angel* (1964) from the Calgary public library shelf. Its characterization from the perspective of a humanized and demonized old woman so permanently affected me that I could no longer look at or think about old people in the same way again. Later, as a graduate student, I was struck in my reading of 1995 Commonwealth First Book Prizewinner Hiromi Goto's *Chorus of Mushrooms* by a similar form, theme, and effect. After a colleague introduced me to Joan Barfoot's *Duet for Three* (1985), which also retrospectively narrates a life from the vantage of old age, I began to think of the three novels together and embarked upon a research project in a manner especially popular at the time—placing an adjective next to body (e.g., female, lesbian, racialized, silent) and adding a category to the corporeal canon. I thought, with aging, that I had found my adjective. I wrote about how fiction from the vantage of elderly female narrators can revise norms of depicting old women as used up, decrepit, asexual, and frail.

Drawing on the perspective of aging bodies in order to approach the study of contemporary Canadian women's fiction aided my understanding of body criticism in general because elderly physical experiences lay bare some crucial assumptions of thinking through the body. Before long, however, I realized that a focus on bodies could ultimately limit my desired theorization of old age. For example, arguing that old bodies could still be sexy, though well intentioned and accurate, to a degree objectifies aging bodies, and this objectification poses particular difficulties for a focus on women's experience of aging. A study encouraging the objectification of female bodies would not meet feminist goals. Also, thinking about aging as primarily physical evades a central argument that, as theorists have argued about disability, old age is a socially constructed phenomenon only partly related to biological change. A balance between physical and other aspects of aging is crucial to transforming current attitudes toward old age. In this book I investigate the mechanisms and effects of constructions of aging in order to combat the automatically negative reactions—the same ones that led me to associate old age with physical change—most readers have to the topic of old age.

This book takes a new approach to tackling the general denigration of the elderly, especially in North America. By turning to contemporary women's narratives and film to counter pervasive media depictions, I chart the revision of cultural narratives of decline. Literature has long been blamed (and unfortunately appreciated) for its capacity to create and promulgate vivid stereotypes. More recently, film has received the same attention. I return to those media to dismantle odious stereotypes that fix old age as a time of disease, decline, and death (usually in that order). It is my ambition to reconfigure the mechanisms that construct old age as primarily negative in order to challenge pervasive attitudes. To that end I concentrate on twentieth-century constructions of elderly women as depicted in mass media and in deliberate artistic constructions, reading those constructions with age as a category of analysis in order to devise new standards and strategies for understanding late life.

Contemporary mass media love to prey on cultural fears of aging, as do many novelists and filmmakers. Directly or indirectly, age affects everyone, and few people want to believe they belong to the category that others and even they deride. There is always someone further along the age continuum to mock and consider vulnerable.[1] Early attempts to make age a central concern in contemporary narrative fiction also pander to cultural fears. Describing age provides authors such as Simone de Beauvoir and Margaret Laurence material to maintain readers' horrified fascination, and, as a result, the authors can expose ageist stereotypes and attitudes even while they perpetuate them to some degree. But depictions of aging do not have to buy into cultural stereotypes of incompetence and disgust. The few constructive depictions of old age that I have found occur mostly in minor, and often minority, contemporary literatures operating at the fringes of what is more culturally acceptable and more widely read. In particular, I have found a larger number of defiant characterizations in recent Canadian production than anywhere else.

Lately gerontologists have begun to think of old age as dialectical, combining seemingly contradictory possibilities such as ineluctable physical change with increased wisdom. A humanities-based approach to aging can consistently maintain the crucial complexity of growing old because works of art, such as literature, can comfortably encompass contradictions and even gain their aesthetic strength from doing so. The interplay between deterioration and mature liberation, what Betty Friedan calls

Janus-faced old age, can be simultaneously complicated and simplified through key narrative elements of characterization, plotting, and narration. Who tells a story of aging affects readers' engagements with that story. Fiction from the perspective of old age frequently pivots on a decision about where an elderly female character should live. The web of personal investments involved in such a decision heightens the complexity of late-life change because a balance must be struck between generational desires and perceived abilities. Autonomy and individuality become increasingly elusive for people on the verge of requiring specific care for physical needs. "Failure" to maintain autonomy is perceived as succumbing to the inevitable "ravages" of age and thereby becoming a social burden. The challenge—which I think fiction is up to—is to individualize old age without diminishing its general import. As my title indicates, however, the individualization of old age invites thinking of aging within a community of women located closer to one end of an age continuum ("older women") rather than maintaining a broader, singular concept of aging ("old woman") as a symbol of late life.

My continual engagement with Laurence's remarkable, nonagenarian protagonist and narrator, Hagar Shipley, enhances not only my attitudes toward the old women around me but also my awe for the power of literary narrative to alter irreversibly my engagement with the social world outside its bounds. It continues to perplex me that an author who has almost as much distance from the experience of old age as I do convincingly renders the internal mechanisms of growing old so that readers can feel newly informed and aware. I remain suspicious that the novel might reflect only a relatively young person's understanding of old age. *The Stone Angel* may simply match my own naive hopes and fears of the process of aging and not accurately construct the inner mind of an old woman. Still, regardless of whether it taps into actual facets of aging, Margaret Laurence's innovative novel makes readers aware of their own thinking about old age and so could change the way in which readers interact with old people they encounter, or at least what they automatically think, subsequent to reading the novel. As readers follow Hagar's reinterpretation of the people around her, they can understand their own reactions to her old age and perceive the shortcomings of their assumptions about old women who seem to resemble Laurence's construction of Hagar.

Usually, when asked about my work, I face scrutiny and skepticism upon revealing that my topic is old age. There are two prevalent responses. One is to question why a young scholar would be interested in such a "depressing" topic. Speakers betray their assumption within that question, and I usually respond by gently revealing that assumption. Old age is too frequently thought of as tantamount to death, but contrary to pervasive habitual thinking, late life is by no means necessarily depressing or gloomy, nor is its study. Through my research I seek to address and eliminate precisely the seemingly automatic, negative association between old age and decrepitude that leads to a prejudice against old people that Robert Butler has named "ageism." The second response consists of an anecdote about an old person known to or observed by the questioner, most often a grandparent. I am often impressed by the influence older relatives have had on people's lives; unfortunately, those anecdotes too often fit into the very modes of describing old age that I wish to illuminate and modify through my work. Elderly uncles are funny because they are deaf; old women are pitiable because they accept help descending bus steps; grandparents make us giggle because they are incongruously sexual. Somehow engagements with old people render younger people so uncomfortable that they must waylay their anguish through humor, pity, and other forms of condescension. Frequent television commercials and comedy skits enhance the sense of incongruity that any change associated with old age evokes. An old woman looking at lacy underwear with interest—very funny; an old couple in Palm Beach baffled by the array of holes they must punch in a newfangled ballot—so pathetic; an old woman curled up in a crib behind her daughter who cannot afford to provide adequate care—so needy.

Despite Robert Butler's coining of the term *ageism* to describe a deep-seated uneasiness on the part of the young and middle-aged, aging does not currently garner the same careful approach as other forms of grouping people (such as gender, ethnicity, and sexuality). For example, even though many comedians make concessions to their audiences according to a general sensitivity to new political demands (often avoiding racist jokes, for example, or at least providing a disclaimer, however ineffective), such consideration does not seem to hold true for the "category" of old age. The Canadian comedy troupe *This Hour Has 22 Minutes,* usually painstakingly aware of inadequate representations, has a repeated spot dedicated to two elderly characters whose entire claim to humor seems to be that younger comedians dress up as "old ladies" and talk. Rarely is their age even the central issue in the skit, but audience members are expected to laugh at the image of old women in dialogue. Even deaf activist/comedian Kathy Buckley, whose work aims to counter senseless stereotyping of disability, feels perfectly comfortable pulling her pants up above her waist to make fun of an aging porter in a routine designed to increase awareness of America's strange paradoxes in dealing with disabilities (October 3, 1998). Most people know somebody further along the age continuum, so comedians do not have to fear, as they do with other forms of stereotyping, that audience members might consider themselves to be the person mocked. In fact, audience members rarely want to think of themselves as old because of the cultural associations that connection generates—though gray pride has begun to catch on in certain small cultural pockets, it has a long way to go to catch up with parallel movements such as gay pride.

I aim to increase awareness of both the stereotyping of the elderly and the reasons that recent cultural and academic movements to eliminate discrimination have largely avoided, or at least left out, old age. Age is primarily a category of analysis in my study, in the way that gender is for feminist studies. I read from the perspective of age studies,[2] and that perspective affects how I perceive age to operate thematically within narrative fiction as well. I begin in the same place as many current theoretical and analytical inquiries. Like postcolonial theory, my analysis of old age seeks to address and deconstruct ill-considered, socially damaging prejudices toward a visible, usually disenfranchised, minority. Like feminism (with which I perceive my project to be in direct dialogue), my analysis of old age grapples with a situation that links people directly to their physical manifestations so that they must think by and through the body both to encounter the world and to be encountered by the world. Also like feminist theory, the study of old age has to carefully negotiate the body, which, although crucial to framing many differences, harbors associations that can impede fruitful avenues of investigation. Like queer studies, age scholarship considers bodies and subjects in a position that one could consider abject and attempts to reimbue that position with a power and authority both necessarily and not necessarily sexual.

Unlike postcolonial, feminist, and queer theory, however, the study of old age is available to most critics with equal critical distance and proximity: Most scholars do not consider themselves old but realize that they will be old given time. I am not someone who could presently be considered old, but old age comprises stages of life I hope to experience.[3] Whereas racial identity is stable for many people (though it can vary geographically and according to myriad cultural contingencies and constructions), and gender or sexual identity frequently also remains stable, age identity changes continuously. Age studies as informed by gender, postcolonial, and queer theory offer a reciprocal advancement because age scholarship elucidates thorny issues such as appropriation and social construction.

Thinking of age as socially constructed, though controversial, follows in the footsteps of numerous academic movements that defy cultural understandings of seemingly physical processes. Disability theorists call this approach *social model theory,* arguing that social structures transform physical differences into impairments. Rosemarie Garland Thomson explains, "Stairs, for example, create a functional 'impairment' for wheelchair users that ramps do not. Printed information accommodates the sighted but 'limits' blind persons. Deafness is not a disabling condition in a community that communicates by signing as well as speaking"

(1997, 7). All of the physical conditions Thomson lists are possible results of aging, but the association between disability and aging does not necessarily occur because of disabilities acquired in late life. People with visible disabilities and people who appear elderly share a battle with cultural interpretations of physical forms that may or may not have much to do with the physical capacity to negotiate restrictive social contexts. To a degree, concrete surroundings and social attitudes determine the parameters of both disability and age.

Physical change is contingent on experience in a complicated relationship to time. Factors such as acquired disability may intervene to change the appearance of age in relation to capacity. Though bodies (usually) change as they negotiate time, there is no necessary physical manifestation of a particular age. Mary Russo raises the perplexing and probing question, "Are we ever only the age we are?" (1999, 25) She pinpoints the difficulty of determining age through any one means, though we often rely on chronology to allow a relational comfort: "A friend of mine, for instance, always sees herself as seven years younger than her sister, whose hair is thinning" (ibid.). Russo's friend interprets physical changes in relation to chronology in order to develop an understanding of age identity, and her understanding will continually move old age away from herself. Another indicator, such as reduced mobility, may replace that of thinning hair in order to continually displace old age from the self.

The construction of age currently involves an interpretation of physical traits thought to signify something culturally. We think a girl cannot be two years old if she does not have any teeth yet and that a woman cannot be seventy if she does not have wrinkles. I hope that understandings of age can grow to include the interpretation of a complex web of factors, including physical change, all of which contribute to the experience of growing older. My analysis mixes with distinction various modes of depiction. I frame my interpretations of written and film narrative with brief discussions of other modes of depiction—such as television representation, medical textbooks, professional photography, academic criticism, and feminist theory—in order to demonstrate the progress I claim fiction and film can contribute to our understanding of the stages of late life and to "reading" the world through language.

This work is interdisciplinary in that it yokes together numerous modes of analysis and description, but it always does so to illuminate narrative fiction, on paper and on film, as a distinct and particular mode.[4] In this study, fiction goes beyond a make-believe construction of a world of possibility and becomes a distinct way of talking about social issues. I argue that it can offer the same kind of conceptual insights as more overtly theoretical modes of discussion but often does so with a wider and more imaginative appeal. I talk mostly about narrative fiction, on paper and on film, because I am interested here in the structures that narrative employs and the means by which narrative imposes order. This is by no means meant to be a comprehensive survey of contemporary fiction about aging. In particular, I argue that narrative fiction, like critical theory, can help in the reevaluation of social problems such as ageism. As a result, it is possible that challenging fictions of aging, those that neither reduce it to a negative physical decline nor banalize it to a simply positive time of peace, can affect social attitudes toward old age. Narrative fiction can go a long way toward reinforcing negative attitudes toward aging and can also defy such attitudes. For this study I have found examples of narrative fiction that I believe fulfill a goal that Aritha Van Herk articulates in her search for "a movement from fiction that deals with the probabilities of our world to its inherent possibilities, a movement toward a fictional imagination that pushes language and idea beyond perception into vision and speculation" (1992, 84). Speaking of narrative fiction written from the perspective of old women, I call this "movement" the *literary potential of old age,* and I intend to tap into the possibilities inherent within narrative forms as well as the possibilities available to old people.

I openly choose to talk mostly about women's experience with old age. Men and women experience aging differently partly because of how they are constructed to perceive self-worth.[5] Old women are perceived to experience at least twofold cultural loss because it is not just their utility but also their femininity that is considered to fade. My choice to talk mostly about women, though, is more complex than this familiar, fundamental consideration. Women typically live longer than men and seem to be more concerned about the issues of extreme late life that I address. I justify my choice by explaining that it is by women and within communities of women that questions of old age have begun to be raised; it is by women and within communities of women that I have discovered constructive depictions of aging; and it is by women and within communities of women that I expect such activism to continue. Further, women typically have responsibility for older people of both genders in terms of providing care and ensuring that care is provided. Frequently, women's expected caregiver status requires them to ensure or provide care for elderly relatives and in-laws, and so they become responsible for aging people even as they comprise the portion of the population that old age affects the most.

Finally, it is late life—latest life—that concerns me here. To a degree, the relevant issues reach back as far as menopause, and I discuss some depictions of middle age, but both serve only as augurs of old age in this study. In keeping loosely with the cutoff point of geriatric medicine, the characters in the narrative fiction I discuss are at least seventy years old and range into their late nineties. Fiction from the perspective of middle-aged women is still remarkable, though reasonably prevalent, and such fiction often begins to address issues of aging similar to the ones I raise here. I find it particularly marvelous that a set of novels and films, most created in Canada, work together to promote diverse new depictions of female aging from the perspective of unquestionably chronologically old women.

By linking an argument about narrative voice with an argument about cultural perceptions of old age, I contend that centering stories on old women contains the potential to challenge damaging stereotypes that currently govern the scripting and prevalent depictions of old women. Narrative has the capacity both to construct and deconstruct, so it can both reinforce and challenge dominant misconceptions of old age. In addition to trying to redeem aging bodies' potential to defy limiting and limited cultural understandings, I now aim to interpret the broad array of signs and symbols of aging as diversely challenging and freeing.

Many people have supported this work. Sarah Westphal introduced me to the viability of old age as a category of analysis and nurtured my interest in the topic. I could not have written this without her encouragement and constant faith. Nicole Markotic's extensive knowledge of body theory and Canadian fiction as well as her attentive edits helped change this from a good idea to a convincing book. Nathalie Cooke's incisive and prompt readings of many sections and her continued support bolstered me through an at times difficult process. In the final stages of revisions, Sherrill Grace provided support, advice, and the kind of knowledge only experience can offer. Sylvia Henneberg and Anne Wyatt-Brown read and made suggestions that both broadened and deepened the book. I am grateful to others who read and commented on early drafts, especially Juliana Abbenyi, Dorothy Bray, Michael Bristol, Robert Lecker, Roxanne Rimstead, and Colleen Shepherd. Many other colleagues supported the work in ways too varied to detail; special thanks go to Laura Hurd Clarke, Hülya Demirdirek, Michael Epp, Ken Madden, John McIntyre, Christine Neufeld, Alan Patten, and Tiffany Potter. My thanks also go to Heather Lee Miller at The Ohio State University Press for the strength of her convictions. I am grateful to McGill University for two major fellowships, to Fonds pour la Formation de Chercheurs et l'Aide à la Recherche for financial support at the doctoral and postdoctoral levels, and to the Social Sciences and Humanities Research Council of Canada for postdoctoral support. Final thanks go to my family, Sue, Tris, and Peter Chivers, for continued support of every kind.

Introduction

Situating Old Women: Fields of Inquiry

The Construction of "Vulnerability"

When the now famous ice storm of 1998 hit Montreal, I lived there alone with my cat. As I sat next to my clock radio, powered by a battery that my neighbor thankfully had on hand, I noticed that I, not yet thirty, fit the prevalent media description of the elderly. The following analysis reflects my resistance to what I perceived, during a stressful time, as the Canadian Broadcasting Corporation's (CBC) attempt to position audience members. The opening section of this chapter describes my impressions of media coverage of an event that affected me personally. I include the impressions here because they set up many key issues of age studies and provide a compelling introduction to the paradox of gender combined with age.

When the reputed "ice storm of the century" swept Quebec, eastern Ontario, and the Northeastern United States, local radio stations leapt to help the millions of potential listeners who could hope to receive information only via battery-powered radio. I spent a few days trapped in my apartment listening to the CBC try to fill round-the-clock broadcast time in the absence of changing conditions to report. Though other English and French radio stations also covered the storm, I, out of habit and maybe even nostalgia, kept my dial tuned to the CBC and became increasingly fascinated by emerging rhetorical patterns. In their indispensable coverage, paradoxes prevailed: Although most people dependent on the broadcast had no electric power in their homes, officials advised them not to venture outside, where sheets of falling ice posed a mortal threat to public welfare, but rather to stay home and watch movies. The same powerless listeners were sternly admonished not to drink the water without boiling it first (an impossibility for those with electric stoves) but above all to remain well hydrated to avoid hypothermia. Such contradictions reveal that announcers and expert guests found it impossible to adjust certain assumptions about their broadcast audience. One reception assumption became gradually and abundantly clear.

As subzero temperatures persisted, listeners heard that although children and the elderly do not shiver when cold, shivering signals a healthy reaction and indicates the body's efforts to maintain heat. If *you* are shivering, the CBC told listeners, *you* are likely not yet suffering from hypothermia. This *you* oddly excluded the one segment of the population about which the CBC, in concert with local authorities, expressed the most concern: the so-called elderly. *You,* the listener, meant somebody roughly between the ages of teenager and sixty (that is, not children or the elderly). Well-intentioned public announcements constantly urged those listeners capable of shivering to check on elderly neighbors. But listeners of *all* ages heard human-interest stories of elderly people who did not want to leave their homes. For example, listeners heard about an eighty-something, forgetful woman who, finally giving in to offers of help, left her home without turning off her stove and caused a fire.[1] In my time listening to the CBC, I never heard a CBC broadcaster say, "If *you* are over seventy, *you* may find that your body does not react the same to extreme cold as it used to." Broadcasters did not appeal directly to the segment of the population about which they exhibited such social concern.

The CBC emergency broadcasts are not exceptional in discourse that condescends to the elderly, but the emergency situation provides a particularly effective context for revealing common late-life stereotypes. What seemed, momentarily, an exciting opportunity for the media spotlight to illuminate numerous positive and negative facets of old age instead predictably manifested countless popular misconceptions. Despite age-old connections between experience and wisdom, the CBC did not consult octogenarians for advice on how to function without electricity—a presumed area of expertise for someone who has necessarily lived through at least one world war and the advent of numerous electrical devices now presumed essential. Of particular note, despite their supposed fragility, the media reported not even one person over the age of sixty who had attempted to heat a home with propane or a hibachi, whereas a number of considerably younger people died as the result of uninformed decisions to heat their homes unsafely. One elderly couple in Notre Dame de Grace (an area of Montreal particularly hard hit by the storm) dug up their old cast-iron cooking implements and, with the help of their gas stove, created radiators to maintain heat in a home that otherwise would have been cold for seven days

(Westphal, personal interview, May 14, 1998). Despite such available anecdotes, CBC radio announcers continually emphasized old people's "fear" of leaving home. Broadcasters attributed this fear to a belief that the same authorities who wished to "save" them would shunt them off to nursing homes and that they would never see their own homes again. Although likely a legitimate concern, the fear of infectious diseases (considerably more dire for those elderly people with deteriorating immune systems) superseded that of lost homes, and indeed an influenza epidemic did sweep through the emergency shelters. Somewhat familiar with managing without electricity, what seventy-year-old woman or man would voluntarily leave home to spend an unknown number of nights in dormitory-style accommodations with young children and inevitable infectious diseases circulating day and night?

CBC's misguided, yet somehow philanthropic, attempts are atypical only in that, during the storm (people lost electrical power for anywhere from two days to three weeks), battery- powered radio provided the main communication link for many people. Otherwise, the network participated in a general media tendency to discuss old age only as a human interest topic and as a phenomenon only loosely related to the target audience instead of as within everyone's either present or (probable) future experience. In the face of a relatively static catastrophe, the CBC had to create for their (in some cases literally) captive audience the drama that people expect from the news. Their choice to "help" those they perceived to be the weakest part of the population allowed them to incite goodwill in listeners who desperately needed not to feel their own need for reassurance. The emergency situation helped stereotypes take over the broadcasts because of a social need to contain and distance the vulnerability that most Montrealers felt. In general, old bodies function as a repository for cultural fears of inadequacy; the Montreal ice storm coverage provides a concentrated example of how that displacement can work.

The inability to project one's own future onto a reading of an old body, or perhaps more properly the inevitability of doing so, results in continued cultural readings of old age as primarily physical, and necessarily physically limited. News coverage such as that of the ice storm concentrates on images and language of vulnerability. Further, wrinkles and other signs of aging often signify that vulnerability culturally. As a result, although they fulfilled a crucial community function, members of the Canadian media reinforced a detrimental image of aging. The all-too-common, but wrongheaded, association of physical deterioration with mental deterioration results in an accompanying refusal to value the necessary experience that comes with old age. Somehow, a body presaging one's own potential physical decline is read as no longer housing the knowledge and background gained while physically more able.

It is not just my research focus that makes me choose primarily examples of women portrayed as feeble and in need. Old women suffer from this association and overvaluation of the physical to an even greater extent than do old men, possibly because of social yearnings to associate the female with the body and the male with the mind.[2] Also, women tend to outlive and so outnumber men in late life, and, of course, the double bind of female gender and old age (famously described by Susan Sontag) whets the cultural appetite for female fragility. On January 13, 1998, shortly after many Montrealers regained their electrical power, the CBC News Magazine aired the shamefully titled "Voices of the Vulnerable." In the segment, women stand in for the incapacity of the elderly, although they are not given the public voice to express their actual capability. The feature deals with the suffering of the elderly during the January ice storm. It fixates on one particular community in Montreal, without specifying this narrow research base. As a result, the report fails to acknowledge the historical specificity of its subjects who live in a Jewish area of Montreal but are all chosen because of their visual match to cultural notions of the elderly. The additional shared cultural factor, beyond age, suggests at least one logical reason—fear of persecution—for the reluctance of these people to leave their homes and be herded into shelters. Because many of the residents are Holocaust survivors, the CBC's representation of stubbornness and lack of understanding could be replaced by one of self-preservation and misunderstanding (Shapiro, personal interview, May 25, 2000).

The feature begins with an image of an elderly woman whom well-intentioned citizens have decided to "rescue": The transcript reads, "I got one down here. I'm sure, potentially, we'll have a problem getting her out. Madame Lacote? Madame Lacote?" Although the rescuers do not bother to specify the problem, they willingly offer the impression that Madame Lacote's physical infirmity adds to her mental stubbornness, rendering her a perfect case for an exposé about humanitarian efforts to assist the misguided. The next "unidentified elderly Montrealer" featured visually matches images of an old woman beset by confusion that, as a voice-over implies, results from the storm-induced trauma. The film clearly demonstrates that in fact she simply cannot hear the directions she has been given to gather her belongings and go into a community room; her confusion plainly results merely from not knowing what the workers are asking her to do. The authorities make no attempt to find a more effective way to communicate with her, possibly because all of their efforts have already been directed toward accommodating the media crews.

Dr. Howard Bergman, a staff member of the Jewish General Hospital, evokes a third image of an old woman to represent the feeble, baffled elderly:

> Let me just give you one example of a lovely 94-year-old lady who's living in an apartment by herself with her cat, getting a lot of help in normal times from her niece, who would come and help with the shopping etcetera. She didn't want to leave because she didn't want to leave her cats; she didn't want to leave her home or possessions. I think the first stress of many of the elderly, besides living through the cold and the uncertainty, was the stress of having to leave their own homes and having to leave sometimes possessions, including a cat.

Not only does Bergman condescend to an old woman to provide an example of "elderly stress," but his example is also largely irrelevant because her experience resembles that of many Montrealers throughout the crisis, along a continuum of age. Elderly women, however tempting the stereotype may be, were not the only Montrealers reluctant to leave pets, companions, possessions, or homes during the ice storm, though they were virtually the only people forced to do so. The choice to situate such a logical and common reaction in an anecdote about someone who matches prevailing cultural notions of weakness, both in terms of gender and age, demonstrates exactly what age (especially when combined with gender) signifies culturally today. The interviewer calls upon Bergman, as an expert, to explain the medical term "elderly stress." Surely, what he describes simply matches the expectations of an audience who may not want to recognize their own habits in those of the "lovely" old woman too attached to her home and cats to venture out into a meteorological disaster.

Notably, though they choose women as visual and anecdotal examples of the fragile old, the CBC News Magazine interviews two old men to perpetuate negative depictions of old women in "Voices of the Vulnerable." Isadore Fogel, speaking of a special shelter for the elderly at the Jewish General Hospital, explains that "there's a blind woman here, maybe I shouldn't mention it, but she—she is very difficult. She yells at the top of her voice with everybody sleeping, and as soon as the people wake up, there's a big lineup of people walking to the bathroom." This embedded narrative demonstrates a member of the already supposedly vulnerable population perpetuating the very attitudes that have resulted in his own coerced removal from home. An interview with Abraham Bonder furthers this tendency when he explains that, although he would not have left his home, "My wife has to go because it's too cold. Much too cold." No one actually interviews old women in the entire piece. As a result, viewers do not even have the opportunity to ascertain whether the tendency to perpetuate pessimistic depictions extends to old women's words. Because they are the only "voices" viewers hear, extending the logic of

CBC's title "Voices of the Vulnerable" leads a critical viewer to conclude that the vulnerable during the ice storm were members of the media and the medical community—they were vulnerable to prevailing stereotypes.

Taken in the spirit it was more likely intended, the title encapsulates the paradox of being female and old. Not only did the supposedly vulnerable have no voice in the coverage, the CBC did not address them directly as potential members of a viewing or listening audience. Because the construction of gender difference relies to a large degree on a specific understanding of women's physical beauty, the implicit cultural question lingers of whether old women can fit into the gender construction of "woman" at all. This subject position, rife with internal tension, becomes an ideal substitute for other cultural tensions and comes to represent what younger segments of society fear. At a time when Montrealers felt and were particularly vulnerable to a devastating weather pattern, the media transferred fear and weakness onto a social group that the remainder of the population could consequently comfort itself by "helping." Those included by the CBC's *you* could patronize those excluded, and younger people had the opportunity to construct superficial strength around a false conception of old people's inevitable dependence. The notion that old women could help not only themselves but also others would threaten a population stabilized through a projected fear and would undermine the feeling of superiority that such a projection had allowed.

I do not mean, however, to condemn entirely media depictions for their problematic and cowardly representations of old age. And the CBC by no means provides the worst examples of the phenomenon of undervaluing elderly people, especially old women. My analysis of CBC ice storm coverage exposes how old age at times substitutes for cultural vulnerability when a scapegoat is needed. This process is unique neither to the CBC nor to the mass media in general. When I contacted the CBC hoping to obtain transcripts of their extensive coverage, Eta Kendall spoke to me with genuine sympathy about "the plight of the elderly" and the resulting "precious moments" (personal interview, October 1998). Many studies of old age also concentrate on vulnerability to examine what is too frequently called, even by Gloria Steinem, "the plight of older women" (quoted in Friedan 1993, 38). Mass media, academic studies, conventional poetry, photography, visual arts, and contemporary humor construct and respond to prior constructions of an expected fragility and a desired, but distanced, incapacity sheltered in the physical frames of recognizably old women. A general, and sometimes even a specialized, public can comfortably pity and even offer help to a group of people who signal physically what they do not desire but have to be careful about possibly becoming.

Body Criticism, Disability Studies, and the Social Construction of Old Age

When academic studies try to address old age, they frequently do so in terms of problem solving, often referring explicitly to "the problem of old age." Of course, many problems do come with late life, as with any stage of human development, but many of the difficulties that old people face result from social (mis)understandings associated with the myriad contingencies of late life. Despite socially created challenges, physical infirmity most frequently presides as the key "problem" automatically associated with old age. The academic specializations clustered around the medical care of old people understandably seek to alleviate the physical infirmities that frequently occur late in life. Medical professionals of course need to recognize that older bodies require specialized care in the same way that extremely young bodies, adolescent bodies, and middle-aged bodies have specific needs. However, it is equally important not to reduce old age *merely* to a physical process because doing so encourages precisely the connections between old age and vulnerability that can do so much damage.

Because late life so often conjures notions of physical infirmity, most people likely think of medicine first as the academic discipline relevant to age studies. And because many physical changes currently accompany late life, medicine is crucial to an understanding of old age. However, because medical language is a scientific discourse, it inevitably classifies and then generalizes in order to diagnose and treat patients. The dominant scientific tradition is reductive in that it tends to explore units before (and sometimes in lieu of) a whole. During old age, when the body is often thought to be paramount, there is increased impetus to consider parts of the body and then the body itself before (and even instead of) the whole experience of old age. Medical language frequently concentrates on the physical, excluding other dimensions of aging and thereby limiting the imaginative framework available for understanding old people. Medical anthropologist Margaret Lock explains that such reductionism "tends to dismiss cultural influences of all kinds, including subjective experience, as superfluous distorting mirrors that disguise the relevant 'facts' waiting to be revealed in the depths of the body" (1993, 370). Medical discourse seems unable to address adequately the full experience of aging because of its limited conceptualization of the body as a composite of interactive units. I would argue further that, for the most part, medical discourse frequently does not value or recognize *narrative* enough to comprehend sufficiently the multifaceted process of growing old. In a standard medical approach, social context and certain kinds of causality obscure rather than create and interpret physical aging.

Counter to medical discourse, the field known as body criticism seeks to incorporate the social and cultural context of the physical in order to understand human experience. Similar to medicine, body criticism also participates in a discourse that needs to generalize and, by doing so, risks abstracting out key differences—Judith Butler's *Bodies That Matter,* for example, are relatively young (1993). Still, her landmark study, though it does not overtly consider the implications of the aging body, provides the possibility to think about how social contexts render aging bodies "abject." As Judith Butler argues, bodies unable to reproduce (lesbian bodies for the purposes of her treatise) can be situated under the rubric "abject." Elderly bodies do not usually exercise sexual desire for the socially sanctioned end of procreation, so any discussion of sexuality and the elderly forces recognition of sexual desire for its own sake. In her study of the female grotesque (which aptly chooses elderly men dressed in drag as a cover photograph), Mary Russo explicitly situates old bodies in the position of the abject by qualifying how the female body can be grotesque with a parenthetical list of grotesque female bodies: "(the pregnant body, the aging body, the irregular body)" (1995, 55). Russo (although only parenthetically) indicates that aging bodies do not fit into paradigms of classical beauty, which is "closed, static, self-contained, symmetrical, and sleek" (8). Though neither theorist fully confronts aging bodies in these early works, both provide tools of analysis for the forces that place aging bodies outside the typical realm of consideration. In the introduction to her edited collection, *Figuring Age: Women, Bodies, Generations,* Kathleen Woodward addresses more directly what she calls the "invisibility" of old women (1999).[3] The ensuing essays focus largely on how social interpretations of physical challenges of old age can cause great personal pain that at times outweighs the more immediate physical pain and thereby contributes to the general denigration of the elderly.

Though body criticism often shies away from aging bodies, those academics who do explicitly discuss the elderly typically focus on the body. Age theorists tend to argue that the body becomes paramount in daily experience during old age. Whatever power the mind may have to influence physical change and whatever cultural narratives may affect concrete experience, aging is currently associated with decrepitude. Because this usually entails a physical decline, a body that lives to old age is (almost always, at this historical moment) eventually (however briefly) circumscribed by its physicality. In her *Aging and Its Discontents,* Kathleen Woodward reads this as foreboding mortality:

> The inevitable and literal association of advanced old age with increasing frailty and ultimately death itself presents a limit beyond which we cannot go. The body in advanced old age not only represents death; it is close to death and will in due time be inhabited by death. The facticity of the mortal vulnerability of the body in old age, and the meanings we attach to it, cannot be explained away by insisting that an ideology of youth, with its corresponding semiotics, is responsible for negative representations of old age. (1991, 18–19)

Most important, she claims that the aging process has a lived reality underscored by bodies' increasing unreliability. Currently, that material process cannot be escaped entirely, but there is also a material reality to a vulnerable newborn that, though it denotes frailty, does not connote the same inappropriate representations. Right now, old bodies do change, but the changes need not be figured *solely* as deterioration. As Woodward implies, the promotion of *positive* aging damages by relentlessly clinging to an impossible, and undesirable, continued youthfulness; this process is called "positive ageism," which, like ageism more generally, results in negative perceptions of what age actually entails by restricting it to false optimism and cosmetic, youthful activity. Susan Wendell's "Old Women Out of Control: Some Thoughts on Aging, Ethics, and Psychosomatic Medicine" draws on a disability studies perspective to explain the difficulties of tackling the physicality of age without reducing the process to decline: "Aging is not always and never *just* being sick or dying, but it is also these" (1999, 135). Whereas positive ageism tries to deny decline altogether, Wendell seeks to incorporate that decline into a larger social process. In dialogue with Margaret Morganroth Gullette's *Declining to Decline,* Wendell contends that "in arguing against the socially constructed midlife decline, it is important, for several reasons, not to insist on its opposite, the 'wonderful' [Gullette's word, on 222 and elsewhere], healthy energetic midlife and old age" (134). The place of the body within age studies is confined, particularly because the choice to think of another or one's self as old usually occurs because of physical appearance. To deny that physicality is to deny most of what makes old age a rich process worthy of academic scrutiny. To pretend that physical changes do not cause physical, social, and emotional pain is to avoid the complexity that offers age studies such potential.

I seek to conceptualize senescence so as to form a basis on which to build new modes of thinking about age and challenge established modes. To do so, I seek cultural depictions that embrace and contribute to the complexity of old age. What I call *constructive* aging brings together positive and negative elements of aging to the extent that it is difficult to determine which is which. The ultimate goal is to trouble the distinction entirely. The physical dimension of old age is a substantial consideration, but it, like numerous other corporeal phenomena, remains open to countless cultural interpretations not simply as an indication of imminent death. We need new stories and readings of growing old.

Currently, wrinkles hold a specific cultural stigma that affects how they are read socially even when they are framed as art. In the January 1991 edition of *Border Crossings,* Montreal photographer Donigan Cumming confronts readers with startling images of a naked, seventy-six-year-old female body. As editor Robert Enright pinpoints in his introduction to the portfolio, a stark opposition to standard pop culture representations (and indeed high art representations) of female nudes ruthlessly prevails. Enright describes various photographs in the following way: "[H]er body in the bathtub, in repose, standing improbably in a sink, is a topography of loss and misdirection—a breast appears like the ear of an old animal; toes are so arthritic they look maliciously broken" (25). "Pretty Ribbons," a portfolio of photographs of Nettie Harris in various states of undress, confronts social understandings of female bodies directly and visually. Harris has an unavoidable visibility that unsettles imaginative stereotypes. Her shocking, naked image confronts viewers with unveiled aged flesh so that they can no longer avoid the stark physical realities of aging. Presented in poses that parody those of young centerfold models, Harris's images suggest a "decrepit" sexuality that threatens popular images of what and which bodies are supposed to be sexy.

Perhaps it is not just that elderly bodies in all their visible disrepair assault aesthetic requirements, but that they speak of what each individual's body could become. Whatever cultural value it could have, Harris's lived experience is visible only to the extent that it is marked on her body, and those markings will be read only in the context of the ageist viewership the photographs confront. Cumming relies on Harris's wrinkles to signify something socially. He could presumably have chosen to enact any number of photographic tricks and indeed may well have. Nonetheless, he chooses to present the photographs as if they are exact representations of an old woman. Viewers accordingly come literally face to face with their preconceived notions of the grotesque aesthetic of age at the same moment that they must confront what "naked woman" usually *signifies* to them. How could a woman agree to display her inappropriate body in this way? What will my body become? Can this woman possibly understand herself to be beautiful?

In his anthropological, historical, literary, and sociological study of how people make sense of their physical world, *The Practice of Everyday Life,* Michel de Certeau suggests that there is something unseemly about a dying body:

> No doubt the part of death that takes the form of expectation has previously penetrated into social life, but it always has to mask its obscenity. Its message is seen in the faces that are slowly decaying, but they have only lies with which to say what they presage (be quiet, you stories of getting old told by my eyes, my wrinkles, and so many forms of dullness), and we are careful not to let them speak (don't tell us, faces, what we don't want to know). (1984, 194)

The "obscenity" of a body presaging death translates into a required (visual) silencing of aged bodies. This is why pictures such as those of Nettie Harris shock viewer expectations—North American society dictates that aged bodies should be covered to allow for a comfortable distancing; they should be prevented from telling "stories of getting old." Too often the narratives typically and automatically associated with old age connect it with death uniformly and without challenge. Cumming's photographs make evident the dangerous assumptions underlying the social position of age because they confront the uniformity of those narratives. Because old age is so often limited to physical deterioration, perceiving that deterioration presents a danger. In order to address and adequately reframe old age as having a particular social and even aesthetic value, "the stories of getting old" have to acknowledge both the physical and the social aspects of aging. New narratives of old age could affect how images of old age come across.

As Wendell's essay evinces, the emerging discipline of disability studies contributes to the rich discourse surrounding bodies to allow for a greater range of experiences and corporealities. Any discussion of aging bodies, like those of any bodies, has to counter norms, because the physical norm is thought to be young, straight, white, able, and male. Disability scholar Rosemarie Garland Thomson, in *Extraordinary Bodies,* has called this norm the "normate," which she defines as "the constructed identity of those who, by way of the bodily configurations and cultural capital they assume, can step into a position of authority and wield the power it grants them" (1997, 8). Though body critics have yet to pay serious attention to aging bodies, much body criticism strips away the many facets of the normate so that eventually body theorists can only reasonably conclude that there is no such thing as a "normal" body, only the compulsion to achieve normalcy. Thomson draws on Erving Goffman to highlight this point: "[T]here is 'only one complete unblushing male in America: a young, married, white, urban, northern, heterosexual, Protestant father of college education, fully employed, of good complexion, weight and height, and a recent record of sports'" (quoted in Thomson, 8). In his foreword to David T. Mitchell and Sharon L. Snyder's *The Body and Physical Difference: Discourses of Disability,* James I. Porter addresses the place of the body. He says, "Averted and silenced, the disabled body presents a threat to the very idea of the body, the body in its pure, empty form. It is this idea that informs the prevailing normativities of the body. And it informs current theoretical views of the body as well" (1997, xiii). Even more than combating a cultural comparison to the yardstick of youth, a study of age has to battle the normative power wielded by the very notion of appropriate bodies. An aging, unreliable body also threatens "the very idea" of a body "in its pure, empty form," which is a youthful body. Expanding Thomson's normate, a goal of disability, postcolonial, queer, feminist, and age studies requires a new reckoning with the forces that construct identity, especially as formed through physicality.

There may be some normative aging bodies—a prescriptive format for aging well—but, in general, the elderly have to fight normalization similarly to people with disabilities and indeed all people. As Wendell argues in *The Rejected Body,* "I imagine that if we did not construct our environment to fit a *young* adult, non-disabled, male paradigm of humanity, many obstacles to nonelderly people with disabilities would not exist" (1996, 19). That is to say, the elderly and people with disabilities alike fight social restrictions and may benefit mutually from successfully challenging them. Contemporary disability scholarship often favors social model theory, which argues, much as feminism argues for gender, that "disability" is constructed whereas "impairment" refers to a less-mediated physical state; the distinction goes beyond terminological appropriateness and, some argue, contributes to a difficult binary opposition. Among others, Mairian Corker and Sally French take issue with the competing terms: "[B]ecause the distinction between disability and impairment is presented as a dualism or dichotomy—one part of which (disability) tends to be valorized and the other part (impairment) marginalized or silenced—social model theory, itself, produces and embodies distinctions of value and power" (1999, 2). Similar to, and even overlapping with, disability earlier in life, old age entails both physical attributes and socially imposed attributes. To focus overly on either is to ignore the lived experience of aging. Wendell elucidates the interaction between the binaristic terms:

> I maintain that the distinction between the biological reality of a disability and the social construction of a disability cannot be made

> sharply, because the biological and the social are interactive in creating disability. They are interactive not only in that complex interactions of social factors and our bodies affect health and functioning, but also in that social arrangements can make a biological condition more or less relevant to almost any situation. I call the interaction of the biological and the social to create (or prevent) disability "the social construction of disability." (1996, 35)

To evade the bodily aspects of aging would be to hide the ways in which those bodily factors interact with social factors to create disabling conditions for the elderly. The instance of aging physicality provides convincing evidence for disability theory's foundation. As with a body without legs, an elderly body is "disabled" only if the signs of aging "mean" something socially. A person in a wheelchair may not be able to navigate stairs, but that is a challenge only in a society that builds stairs rather than ramps. A person who appears elderly may not win a beauty contest but only in a society with youthful standards for beauty. As note 3 describes, sixty-five-year-old Barbara Macdonald is asked to leave a Take Back the Night march, or rather her younger lover is asked on her behalf, because Macdonald looks as though she will not be able to march—she appears unable because of what her physicality signifies, not because she cannot walk ("Look Me in the Eye"). The idea that age is socially constructed troubles some people because of the seemingly unavoidable physical problems that come with age and because the term "constructed" is sometimes taken to imply complete creation, rather than a social manipulation of available physical material. To say that old age is socially constructed or determined is not to deny the materiality of hot flashes or wrinkles. Social construction involves how physicality relates to, or, as Wendell puts it, interacts with, a social environment, either concrete, as in prohibitive stairs, or intangible, as in the discourses and images of the beauty industry.

Age shows on the body, and others interpret that age as signifying a number of usually negative changes that pervade more than just physical aspects of life. In *Old Age,* Simone de Beauvoir convincingly argues that those interpretations determine self-acceptance of age identity: "In our society the elderly person is pointed out as such by custom, by the behaviour of others and by the vocabulary itself: he is required to take this reality upon himself" (1977, 324). She initiates the scholarly position that age is a social construction and argues that a reckoning with age involves absorbing social values. Overly focusing on the constructedness of the fragility of age, however, risks evading the physical changes that currently govern late life and discourses of late life and that have to be reckoned with to provide the "frail old" with full access to social resources. A more encompassing dialectical gerontology, as Harry Moody proposes,[4] insists upon a mutual recognition of physical and social signs of aging and upon a reciprocal exchange between science, social science, and humanities scholars to defy existing damaging narratives of aging. Such combinations may be able to alter interpretations of aging bodies and thereby to rewrite and reread pervasive narratives of old age.

Pervasive Narratives of Aging and Margaret Lock's "Myths of Menopause"

Medical anthropologist Margaret Lock's *Encounters with Aging: Mythologies of Menopause in Japan and North America* addresses one way that narrative can contribute to the study of aging (1993). Her methodology provides an important model for age studies, and her focus on Japan provides a helpful introduction to a study of North American aging because scrutiny of one culture's constructions of aging can help to make those of one's own appear strange. Although it might be more difficult to identify cultural attitudes from within a cultural framework, witnessing their effect "outside" one's own milieu can aid analysis "within." Lock's experiences in Japan clarify how physical signs of aging take on specific significance that depends on cultural context. Nettie Harris's photographs, for example, might signify differently outside North America.

When Lock questions the supposed universality of menopause, she presents personal narratives cumulatively so that they reinforce the cultural dimension they illustrate. She solidly grounds *Encounters with Aging* in skeptical scrutiny of pervasive Western medical discourse and the historical progression of misogynist paradigms of female midlife. To justify her criticism of such dominant viewpoints, she presents preview excerpts and then entire interviews with Japanese women. The initial excerpts highlight passages in the later entire narratives, grouped by subjects suggested by the preceding selections, so that an overall trajectory develops out of themes arising from the (translated) words of Japanese women. She then compares the narrative patterns with current data about aging in North America. Lock's explicit theoretical grounding for her decision to incorporate personal narratives claims that medical language neglects key aspects of human experience: "What people experience and report in connection with their bodies is not in essence the same kind of information produced through observation, measurement and abstraction" (xxiii). Because neither medical language nor any other discourse, according to Lock, sufficiently describes experiences of human bodies, "human beings create narratives to express the relations between biology, individual sentience, culture and history" (373). For her study, narratives reflect human experience, and so personal narratives necessarily differ from and resist the sweeping generalizations that the biological emphasis of medical language makes possible and even necessary: "Narratives of subjectivity do not permit broad generalizations and abstractions but encourage instead a contextualisation of specific pieces of the puzzle and provide a very important constraint on the way in which we obtain and interpret biological and statistical information" (xxxix–xl). Personal narratives not only enable and enforce individuality in the study of physical processes, they also impose order on how nonnarrative information, or data, comes across. First-person descriptions of experience can influence the ways in which other individuals receive and understand their own bodies. In a search for new stories and readings of aging (though not quite old age) in Japan, Lock turns to individual personal narratives.

Konenki, a Japanese word roughly—though not at all exactly—analogous to menopause, denotes a phase unwelcome not so much because of what it threatens in itself but more as "an augury for the future, as a sign of an aging and weakening physical body" (14). Lock claims, "Several Japanese women state explicitly that *konenki* is the beginning of old age (*roka gensho*) and, although having little significance as such, can be a potent sign for the future" (44). The period of middle age usually marked by *konenki* represents a new relationship with old age in that, rather than sentimentally longing for a golden past, Japanese women "choose to focus much more on human relationships, and the way in which in middle age, a woman turns from being concerned primarily with children and their care to enjoy a brief spell of relative freedom ('mother's time of rebellion'), before she becomes fully occupied with the care of aged people for a good number of years" (45). The impending care of old people during a partly physical transition—*konenki*—underscores how the aging process is central to these narratives. Women are responsible for the care of the elderly in traditional Japanese culture, in which most women of this generation continue to participate. Even in the brief period of time when they are not responsible for caring for others, *konenki* often makes them aware of the old age they will experience both second- and firsthand. This awareness pervades their personal narratives.

Though not overtly about old women, Lock's study demonstrates how middle age anticipates old age for Japanese women. Lock writes about women between forty-five and fifty-five years of age in terms of their placement in a Japanese temporal schema related to empires (e.g., Meiji, Shōwa). She implicitly demonstrates the historical specificity of aging and at the same time explicitly explores its cultural specificity. The shōwa hitokawa women (born in the first decade of the Shōwa reign [1926–1988]) whom she interviews lived through the Second World War and take pride in having survived that difficult time. Those in traditional situations and married to eldest sons usually adjusted to household lives under the scrutiny and control of a meiji (1868–1912) mother-in-law. Repetition among the women's narratives suggests that the shōwa hitokawa women have found such domestic adjustment difficult. However, patterns emerge throughout their stories indicating that they generally believe they lead easier lives than their mothers, they still expect to take care of their elderly parents-in-law, yet they do not expect the same care from their own offspring or offsprings' spouses. Different women of the same generation often express and emphasize these three key points. Despite such shared specific cultural and historical experience, the individual narratives of such women, when interviewed about *konenki,* vary dramatically.

Lock articulates a pervasive myth of *konenki* that (as with nineteenth-century British notions of leisurely bourgeois women with too much time on their hands for reading fiction) figures as lazy housewives middle-aged women who succumb (or admit) to the physical symptoms of *konenki.* Traditionally, Japanese people perceive physical complaints as excuses for not conforming to standards of discipline and continual work. None of the women Lock interviews show even glimmers of matching that circulating denigration of physical and other changes at midlife (i.e., none are lazy housewives). Still, women experiencing middle age in Japan listen to a generally applied story that works as an ideological tool and influences their own descriptions of personal experiences: "[T]he rhetoric thus becomes a yardstick against which women measure and from which they dissociate themselves but also produces a stereotyped specter of the archetypal disciplined Japanese woman fallen from grace, a specter that helps to keep Japanese women divided among themselves and insensitive to the reality of one another's lives" (106). The false tale of the lazy housewife controls, in that it gives order to, the way that women describe their own experiences of *konenki* in relation to the lazy housewife figure. Even if one woman knows that her physical experience does not result from a desire to shirk responsibility, she will likely be reluctant to admit to anyone what will probably be perceived as a shortcoming. The cultural silence reduces the chance that women will discover other narratives of *konenki.* Any sign of succumbing to physical change—of not continuing to work hard or feel good—signals failure because it *seems* to match the lazy housewife story. Consequently, a feeling of inadequacy accompanies any acknowledgement of midlife change, and this feeling prevents women from gathering together and learning that the archetype is only that and does not have to pose a threat to individual experience.

Lock's methodology reveals a common tendency among Japanese women to speak about certain elements of *konenki* while remaining silent about others. The layering of narratives allows her to apply the literary device of theme to a broad survey of disciplines so that she can pick out the relevant threads according to the repetitions and weave them together to demonstrate a significant cultural specificity in a phenomenon previously considered universal. Lock turns to narrative to examine the full experience of aging—in her case, middle age. Her findings are impressive and counter medical beliefs that a diet high in fish and soy accounts for Japanese women's *konenki*. It is possible that a pervasive cultural narrative that characterizes *konenki* symptoms as shameful also prevents even the naming of hot flashes. It is also possible that the vastly different cultural role of women between the ages of forty-five and fifty-five results in a physical phenomenon distinct from that of North American women in the same age group. Lock determines at the very least that this physical experience is defined, if not caused, by cultural context. The personal narratives and their relationship to circulating narratives about aging contribute to a new theory of the aging process. Lock determines which narratives participate in the construction of aging in order to discover how to undermine or transform those narratives. Her work presents one example of how a recent emphasis on narrative offers social scientists an innovative and effective approach to reexamining social processes.

Narrative and Humanities Age Scholarship

The field dedicated to reexamining the social process of old age, gerontology, is beginning to attract some humanities scholars who will surely enhance its interdisciplinarity and contribute greatly to the role narrative can play in understanding the elderly. The theoretical, methodological, and applied facets gerontology rely heavily on observed data and thereby, despite Clark Tibitts's development of social gerontology, tend toward a fact-based, body-centered study (Kart 1990, 21). As James Birren says, "we [gerontologists] are in a phase of being data-rich and theory poor" (quoted in Achenbaum 1995, 20). Thomas R. Cole and Ruth E. Ray explain in the introduction to their *Handbook of the Humanities and Aging*, "Gerontological knowledge making remains dominated by the paradigm of modern science and its various expressions in the social and medical sciences" (2000, xi). Humanities-based gerontology, which includes literary gerontology, may be able to fill the theoretical gap Birren perceives because it provides opportunities to piece together the myriad facets of aging into a complex cultural picture. Because artistic works, including literature, rely on complexity for their aesthetic value, their study can maintain the many seemingly contradictory facets of old age. As I state in the preface, narrative, for example, can offer a perspective on aging that avoids categorizing late life as either positive or negative and that balances its physical and social elements. Literary analysis of narrative offers a rich reconfiguration of old age equal to the complexity of narrative depictions of the elderly.

In part because they often draw on autobiographical theory, in part because they frequently write about autobiography, and in part because of an inevitable compelling personal investment in aging, North American humanities age scholars tend to write themselves into their work. In doing so they often reveal an anxiety about what some euphemistically call the "coming of age." Even when not writing explicitly autobiographical essays, critics explore their own personal experiences with age or with the age of loved ones. Kathleen Woodward's recent anthology, *Figuring Age: Women, Bodies, Generations,* exemplifies the autobiographical tendency within age scholarship. The interdisciplinary collection of essays seeks to make older women more "visible" in order to reflect on the process of growing older (1999, xvi). To achieve these goals, scholars write themselves into essays about subjectivity, historicity, psychoanalysis, visuality, performance, family, and age.

In "The Marks of Time," Nancy Miller makes her aim explicit: "I want to speak of aging as a project of coming to terms with a face and a body in process—as an emotional effort, an oscillation that moves between the mirrored poles of acceptance and refusal" (1999, 4). Focusing on the face, Miller offers devastating explanations of her own and other women's reactions to their own age. Miller's resolution to the painful dilemma presented by her own image acknowledges, if only questioningly, a strong social influence on interpretations of aging. She resists the pervasive cultural stories of aging, and she incites readers to reevaluate and rewrite cultural narratives to make room for new understandings of physical and other change: "[P]art of how to find new ways of perceiving ourselves as aging bodies and faces is to construct a narrative in which these images can be read, otherwise" (12). In her contribution, "Scary Women: Cinema, Surgery, and Special Effects," Vivian Sobchack acknowledges the luxury that allows her, and other contributors, to reflect on her own physical aging as she writes about rejuvenation technologies (1999). Similar to Miller, she speaks of her distaste for her changing face and, going a step further, acknowledges her struggles over the option of cosmetic surgery. As does Miller, Sobchack draws on her own face to reinterpret the cultural significance of age so that, given time, she will not turn away from the mirror. Patricia Mellencamp begins her contribution, "From Anxiety to Equanimity: Crisis and Generational Continuity on TV, at the Movies, in Life, in Death," with a personal narrative in which she describes the moment she became "an old woman" in her own and in others' eyes (1999, 310). Kathleen Woodward's own contribution to her collection, "Inventing Generational Models: Psychoanalysis, Feminism, Literature," opens with a narrative that recollects childhood encounters with her grandmother. She remembers herself as a child connecting with the older woman via objects that evoked shared stories, and, as an adult, she identifies the relationship as one that is absent from Freudian psychoanalysis. She later draws on her own experience with aging to dismiss models she, as a younger woman, found more valuable and turns to literary models that she, in light of her own aging, finds more "suggestive" (1999, 155).

As evidenced by these examples from *Figuring Age,* personal narratives have enormous potential to address perceptual gaps left by inadequate academic and media depictions of aging.[5] Autobiographical accounts can challenge circulating narratives that depict aging as simplistically negative or straightforwardly noble, and they often refuse a straightforward concentration on either physical or social aspects of growing old, demonstrating poignantly how intimately linked the two can be. The authors I cite each struggle to reconcile their sense of self with their sense—mediated by social strictures—of their aging physical being. As a result, one of Woodward's collection's greatest strengths is that although it is by no means an entirely *positive* contribution to age studies, it is an almost entirely *constructive* one. It provides a basis for new and challenging ideas about aging. When Woodward articulates the goals of *Figuring Age,* she explains that narrative has a role to play in changing social attitudes toward old women: "The purpose of this book is to help bring the subject of older women into visibility and to reflect on growing older as women, with our contributions to this project built primarily on the foundation of stories and images, words and visual texts" (1999, xvi). She consistently turns to narrative to make her introductory points, recounting three stories (one about the accidental death of eighty-six-year-old Anna Gerbner, one about an abused eighty-seven-year-old widow, and one about activist Maggie Kuhn's meeting with Gerald Ford) in the first four pages of her introduction. I agree that to develop the "new ways of thinking about growing older" (xvi) Woodward overtly seeks, narrative must be a chief object of study. Autobiographical narratives certainly can contribute—and have done so—to the process of increasing awareness and complex understanding of late life, and I think overtly fictional narratives have another, equally important, contribution to make.

Both reading and viewing (though likely more the former than the latter) narrative fiction provide an opportunity to engage with age that at first still seems to evade old bodies. There is of course a profound difference between an actual old person and a depiction of an old person, even when an aging actor embodies that depiction. An engagement with a text is, as Thomson points out when discussing disability, static compared with the dynamic engagement required with a living person. And, as Thomson argues for disability, in a typical representation of an old person, age often stands in for the whole person, disallowing the complexity sometimes achieved through an engagement with the full, lived reality of age. However, because age can always be displaced along a continuum, and because age alarms many people who fear their own future, an engagement through narrative fiction might be a gentler and therefore potentially more successful way to begin the process of dismantling harmful attitudes. Atypical representations of old people in fiction and film allow readers and viewers a new approach to addressing old age; such an entrance may lead to the conclusion that typical representations of frailty, poverty, and nagging are as mythical as the lazy housewife story that Lock claims controls *konenki* in Japan.

Larry Polivka has probably best expressed what humanities scholars give to gerontology. At the 1994 "Aging and Identity: A Humanities Perspective" interdisciplinary conference in Florida, he answered a question about what of practical value humanists can contribute: In his opinion "the humanities can help older people to understand the narratives of their own lives and can also assist gerontologists and others who work with the elderly in their efforts to preserve their clients' dignity, identity, and self-worth" (quoted in Deats and Lenker 1999, 11). Reevaluating narratives of aging—both circulating and more overtly constructed in the form of literature and film—provides a new vantage point on what is inevitable to late life and what is imposed from without. Literary scholars analyze patterns of and within such narratives and can do so with an eye to maintaining an image of aging that entails a complex array of physical, social, and cultural factors. To me, and I think to Polivka, narrative is not merely a resource to be mined to determine and test cultural attitudes toward the elderly. Narrative provides the clues to the creation of the stereotypes that fix old age as a time of decline. I contend that it also contains clues to the revision of those ways of thinking. And it has the advantage of being able to rethink late life from various vivid perspectives rather than reducing it in a way that almost always leads to negative generalizations. Even applied to physical dimensions of aging, narrative offers the potential to avoid pitfalls—such as essentialism, appropriation, and relativism—that many current theoretical movements have difficulty negotiating.

When sociologists Jon Hendricks and Cynthia A. Leedham introduce a scholarly volume titled *Perceptions of Aging in Literature,* they explicitly turn to what they call in a subtitle "Literature as a Data Base" (1989). Literary analysis holds extraordinary potential for enriching gerontological study, but the examination of a wide cultural, temporal, and generic range of literary works as "a highly select and specialized data set" does not quite capture what literary scholars, including those published in this volume, can achieve (3). In the preface, Andrew Achenbaum writes, "More than other types of inquiry into aging, humanistic gerontology has emphasized the extent to which modes of conceptualizing and expressing ideas have perennially shaped our viewpoints and conditioned our behavior" (xiv). Humanities scholars who have turned to age studies, rather than merely mining cultural products for evidence of attitudes toward the elderly, have exposed theories of—"modes of conceptualizing"—old age, opening the door for new models. They acknowledge and encourage the social construction of age and work toward understanding the processes behind it. In particular, literary gerontology can balance social and cultural narratives of aging with the physical dimensions of aging to develop rich models for new understandings of late life.

The paradigmatic potential of narrative suggests that stories might provide a way to reconceptualize old age and counter models of decline without flattening old age into merely positive aging. In *Cinema and Spectatorship,* Judith Mayne explains, "The common interface between narrative and psychoanalysis suggests that the act of storytelling needs to be understood as one of the most fundamental ways in which one constructs an identity, in both cultural and individual terms" (1993, 24). For her it is not just what narrative chooses to represent, but also the process narrative enacts that makes it a significant field of study. Narrative can guide how old age is seen, heard, felt, and understood. Woodward has explored this process within common narratives of psychoanalysis in her *Aging and Its Discontents* (1991). Personal narrative can contribute further to the process because it is grounded in experience and so has credibility and even appeal. Barbara Frey Waxman chooses, in her second book about narrative and aging, *To Live in the Center of the Moment,* to write about "self-consciously literary autobiographies" because "[t]hey are . . . potentially more transformative of sociopolitical attitudes about aging because of their sophisticated narrative methods, depth of characterizations, and rich descriptive powers. In other words they are more capable of creating 'literary experiences' for readers, more skilled at transporting readers into the foreign country of age" (1997, 17). She compares what she calls "literary autobiography" with autobiography by authors who have not had careers as writers. In choosing to focus on literary authors, she has begun to discover personal narratives that work as new models for the narration of old age. Her reason for selecting those writers is similar to my reason for concentrating on narrative fiction. I examine precisely the "sophisticated narrative methods," especially narrative voice; the "depth of characterizations," in particular of the narrative agent; and the "rich descriptive powers" enacted by narrators of overtly fictional narratives about old age. Those narrative elements compel a reevaluation of old age, which, to borrow (like Waxman) from May Sarton, is frequently a foreign country, so that readers might transform their "sociopolitical attitudes." I do not mean to suggest that reading narratives of aging provides readers with the experience of aging. Rather, narratives of old age can offer ways of thinking about the experience of late life that *could* change how readers interact with the elderly and with themselves as they age. Narrative fiction deserves scrutiny in this regard because it engages readers on slightly different premises than do overt personal narratives. Further, the rich investment in language that literary forms require provides fertile ground for the revision of the strong cultural narratives that otherwise might make age a frightening, or at the very least, an uninteresting topic.

Gerontological study as a whole grapples with the major challenge of how to balance the individuality of the aging process with the generalization that an interdisciplinary field of study encourages. Narrative fiction holds a particular potential for theorizing old age because of its capacity to work with vivid individual examples that remain individual while relevant to a wide range of experience. When Margaret Laurence develops the character of Hagar Shipley, she does not merely offer readers an example of an elderly woman. She offers an imaginative embodiment of social constructions of aging that gains some strength from the fact that it is entirely fictional. Nobody could argue that Hagar Shipley exemplifies old women in Canada, but it is possible to argue that she operates as a metaphor for the multiple, shifting meanings that age takes on within a larger social world. Even if that reading does not quite hold, Hagar figuratively and vividly embodies many of the concerns that old women harbor without pretending to speak for them as a community. She achieves the individuality frequently evaded by considerations of aging, yet her depiction is widely applicable.

The Literary Potential of Old Age

This study is based very much on potential. At this historical moment it is still subversive to imply that old age is a time of enormous potential—the words "old age" and "possibility" seem incongruous when linked. It is not so extraordinary to claim that literature holds a vast potential to transform a larger social world. I want to examine the potential within literary narrative in combination with the potential inherent within old age. To connect these two concepts, that narrative holds a world of possibility and that old age does as well, I suggest the possibility of a type of reading that is, as Waxman puts it, transformative. Theories of readership, and in its turn spectatorship, have examined myriad, often related, scenarios for the engagement with text (written or film) and its effect on audience. Wolfgang Iser's allowance for a number of readings that occur somewhere between implied and actual readers, Roland Barthes's coded reader, David Bleich's subjective reader, and Stanley Fish's interpretive communities, to name a few, have more recently given way to politically charged, contextually based arguments (particularly in postcolonial criticism) that challenge the precepts of dominant literary forms. To a large degree, my argument rests on later, more ideological, arguments because the literary potential of old age depends upon the ideological positioning of readers.[6] This work depends upon the postcolonial arguments that readers come to texts with a set of assumptions that they try to impose upon the texts and that those assumptions can (and in some instances should) be oppositional. The ensuing chapters explore, with a different category of analysis (age), the possibilities that an interaction between text and reader can help to construct new narratives and new theories of aging.

I am most interested in how author, text, and reader can come together in a conjunctive process, what I call "committed reading," that could transform the way the text operates in the future and the way the reader understands both it and a larger social world. Conventional reader response theory tends to concentrate necessarily on the synchronic reading process rather than on the diachronic social process *begun* by the act of reading. One goal of this study is to suggest some ways in which reading and viewing narrative can contribute to forms of profound thinking and social practice that extend beyond engagement with the text. I am most interested in what reading can yield. This book enacts my own committed reading and will, I hope, contribute meaningfully to ongoing efforts to theorize how damaging understandings of old age might be countered with more constructive accounts. What happens when we turn to a novel or a film as we turn to theory and look to it for a profound rethinking of a social problem[7] depends in part on the particular reader and the nature of the reading in question, and it also depends to a large degree on the complexity and tenor of the text in question.[8]

Gary Saul Morson draws on the work of Mikhail Bakhtin to make the strong claim, "Critics and intellectual historians have overlooked *that literary genres are themselves profound forms of thinking*. The most important content of literature is not to be found in explicit statements nor even in a given work's import, however profound. We must not miss the wisdom carried by genres themselves" (1999, 175). According to Morson, what defines the novel as a genre (for Bakhtin) determines its import in terms of critical thought. The form of the novel and its relationship to a social fabric are crucial to its rhetorical impact. As Ken Hirschkop puts it, "So far as Bakhtin is concerned, logical argument belongs to the world of rhetoric and direct discourse, a world inhabited by disembodied ideas. The novel's procedures, by contrast, present arguments in a different form, in the belief that this fictional experiment can reveal the import and significance of ideologies more adequately than could pure verbal disputation" (1989, 27). The novel to some degree embodies ideas, even if they are embodied by constructed speakers (such as characters and narrators) as much as by the putative author. In "The Race for Theory," Barbara Christian argues that such an embodiment results in the complexity that I claim is necessary to a constructive approach to age studies: "Writers/artists have a tendency to refuse to give up their way of seeing the world and of playing with possibilities; in fact, their very expression relies on that insistence. Perhaps that is why creative literature, even when written by politically reactionary people, can be so freeing, for in having to embody ideas and recreate the world, writers cannot merely produce 'one way'" (1988, 75). The structure of literary production, its need to embody ideas, provides the literary potential of old age in that the multiplicity that both Bakhtin and Christian explain allows for a conceptualization of aging that neither denies nor misrepresents the lived body in late life.

In order for the novel as a genre to have the potential for which Bakhtin and some of his followers argue, it must have a particular impact on at least committed readers. Bakhtin recognizes that the situation of reading makes the novel unique, explaining in "Epic and the Novel," "Of all the major genres only the novel is younger than writing and the book: it alone is organically receptive to new forms of mute perception, that is, to reading" (1981, 3). One could make a similar claim about film and viewers, and the process of embodiment is even more vivid (and double) in that mode since the constructed speakers within a film are embodied physically as well as textually (in that actual actors play them). Thus, theories of readership to some degree can apply to spectatorship, and theories of spectatorship (which I discuss further on) can similarly apply to reading.

In "Discourse in the Novel," Bakhtin sketches out a theory of the reader that is generally thought to be inadequate and incomplete. He explains, "The listener and his response are regularly taken into account when it comes to everyday dialogue and rhetoric, but every other sort of discourse as well is oriented toward an understanding that is 'responsive'—although this orientation is not particularized in an independent act and is not compositionally marked" (1981, 280). He claims that drawing on dialogue as a model to understand other modes of expression entails an understanding not just of speech but also of response, and the combination of the two composes utterance. David Shepherd argues that a slippage between speaking and writing makes dialogism crucial to how Bakhtin conceptualizes the reader, characterized as the listener through much of his writing. As Shepherd puts it,

> However, the constant sliding throughout the essay ["Discourse in the Novel"] between speaking and writing, listener and reader, although it leads to a certain theoretical fuzziness, actually goes hand in hand with an unremitting emphasis on the dependence of dialogism on a context which is crucially not intratextual, but external to the enclosure of the text: "every word smells of the context or contexts in which it has lived its socially intense life, all words and forms are inhabited by intentions" (DN 293). (1989, 84)

The investment of the novel in the "maximal zone of contact" and the way in which each word is overlaid with layers of preexisting social significance encourages Bakhtin's articulation of the reader as listener. The concept of the reader-text relationship as dialogue begins to address not just the reading process but also the process *begun* by reading. A reader brings a particular context to bear on a novel, and, to extend the implications of Bakhtin, the same reader might bring different aspects of a historical context to bear on the same novel in a rereading.

Though what he means by it remains unsuitably vague, Bakhtin desires an active reader as opposed to an unengaged one and proposes that reading participates in the process he elucidates: "To some extent, primacy belongs to the response, as the activating principle: it creates the ground for understanding, it prepares the ground for an active and engaged understanding. Understanding comes to fruition only in the response. Understanding and response are dialectically merged and mutually condition each other; one is impossible without the other" (1981, 282). This process makes the reader, and especially the reader's assumptions, crucial to dialogism. Further, it provides the possibility for the type of constructiveness I mention, in that a response to a text provides the basis or "creates the ground" for an engaged understanding. For example, thinking about old age as a response to reading the characterization of Hagar Shipley makes it possible for me to have an active and engaged understanding not only of *The Stone Angel* but also of the social context into and out of which it is written. This is a second type of dialogism that overlaps with the more commonly understood dialogism: "This new form of internal dialogism of the word is different from that form determined by an encounter with an alien word within the object itself; here it is not the object that serves as the arena for the encounter, but rather the subjective belief system of the listener" (282). In separating out the forms of dialogism, which elsewhere, Bakhtin explains, become intertwined for an interpreter of text, Bakhtin makes the ideological positioning of the reader crucial to the encounter between author, text, and reader. Shepherd claims, "What is important at this point is that when Bakhtin is introduced into the specific area of reader-oriented theory, this brings us ineluctably to acknowledge those questions of politics and ideology which are bracketed out, consciously or otherwise, by theorists such as Iser and Fish" (101). Bakhtin's conceptualization of the reader provides the basis for an understanding of a committed engagement with a text. However, what Bakhtin does not emphasize, and what I believe to be crucial, is how a novel might affect a reader's subjective belief system, so that one novel might become part of the context a reader brings to another novel or even to the same novel at a later date.

Judith Mayne's work on cinema and spectatorship explains more clearly how one work can contribute to the perception of another. She claims that "spectatorship is not just the relationship that occurs between the viewer and the screen, but also and especially how that relationship lives on once the spectator leaves the theater" (1993, 2). Mayne addresses what she perceives as the main problem within the historical evolution of criticism on cinema and spectatorship: an attempt to divide or unify opposing notions such as "passive" versus "critical," "subject" versus "individual," "dominant" versus "marginal," "social" versus "psychic," and "woman" versus "women." Her term *spectator* intends to evoke the difficulty of distinguishing between or eliding the ideas of the "subject" and the "viewer." As she puts it, "I am opposing, in other words, the cinematic *subject* and the film *viewer* so as better to situate the *spectator* as a viewer who is and is not the cinematic subject, and as a subject who is and is not a film viewer" (36). The term *spectator* encompasses the various ways in which people might come to a text, as critic or as fan, for example and, perhaps more important, the ways in which people might leave a text.[9]

Spectatorship as Mayne describes it allows for contradictory and changing personal views that may or may not accompany different viewing experiences. She confesses, "Spectatorship is one of the few places in my life where the attractions to male adolescence and feminist avant-garde poetics exist side by side. For Chantal Akerman's particular approach to spectatorship, for instance, engages me in different but equally satisfying ways as Arnold Schwarzenegger's" (3). A study of spectatorship allows for a complex process that, like reading, contains and even gains strength from its internal tensions. As Mayne puts it,

> Here is another level of complexity, for spectatorship may find its most condensed forms in the cinema, but spectatorship is not reducible to the cinematic. For many scholars working in film studies, the study of spectatorship has provided a way to understand film in its cultural dimension, while avoiding the simple determinism of the reflection hypothesis, whereby films "show" or reflect in relatively static ways the preoccupations of a given society. Instead, the study of spectatorship involves an engagement with modes of seeing and telling, hearing and listening, not only in terms of how films are structured, but in terms of how audiences imagine themselves. (32)

The process of spectatorship, like the process of reading, expresses (even embodies) how audiences develop self-understanding. The form of narrative fictions encourages an engagement not just with a representation of a particular social moment but also with a distinct mode of conceptualizing it. For example, in viewing *The Company of Strangers,* audience members do not merely learn how old women are treated in Canada; rather, they both witness and participate in the ways in which stories of aging, and attitudes toward it, are formed. The very dynamism of that engagement provides a potential for the reconfiguration of social attitudes, such as ageism.

Mayne's most important observation for the future study of spectatorship and reading is that it is impossible to separate out a radical viewer from a complicit viewer. The delicate and pleasurable imbrication of complicity and resistance defies film theory's past attempts to characterize spectatorship as defined by *either* subjects *or* viewers. It also counters reader-response theory's claims that readers must be *either* active *or* acted upon. In her updated *Narratology,* Mieke Bal defends and explains her own continued engagement with narratology by saying, "What I propose we are best off with in the age of cultural studies is a conception of narratology that implicates text and reading, subject and object, production and analysis, in the act of understanding. . . . A theory, that is, which defines and describes narrativity, not narrative; not a genre or object but a cultural mode of expression" (1997, 222). Escaping the binaries of most structuralist narratological studies, Bal's narrativity changes the coordinating conjunction of exclusivity—"or"—to that of inclusivity—"and." I situate my study precisely within that conjunction so that I offer an examination of how the author of fiction about old age makes an appeal to the audience who might engage with or commit to that piece of art. That commitment can alter subsequent readings of the same or different texts. The question for me is not whether to privilege the author, the text, or the reading but how to link all three in an examination of two cultural phenomena: narrativity and old age.

In what follows I invest in a group of contemporary fictional narratives centered on old women as a committed reader seeking to benefit from the aesthetic and topical complexity of the works, examining both what the texts offer and how an encounter with them may influence what Bakhtin calls the "zone of maximal contact." Following Janice Rossen, Barbara Frey Waxman, and Anne Wyatt-Brown's lead, I examine narrative fiction's particular role in addressing the social problem not of old age, but of negative perceptions of old age. Wyatt-Brown and Rossen explore how aging affects creativity, as Wyatt-Brown puts it, in order to "challenge the preconceptions about aging that influence our thinking about later life" (1993, 3). The study combines personal narratives with the creation of fiction and poetry to examine how the experience of aging affects the production of literary worlds; they focus on creativity in late life. Barbara Frey Waxman's *From the Hearth to the Open Road: A Feminist Study of Aging in Contemporary Literature* concentrates on popular journalism and novels (including short stories) about three middle- to late-life stages (1990, 40–60; 60–84; 85ff.). She is especially concerned with how the works affect readers, arguing that they "create a receptive readership for more complex fictions of aging" (12). Those more complex fictions of aging are the focus of my current study, which moves beyond the printed page to include what I call the silvering screen. I continue the work of Rossen, Waxman, and Wyatt-Brown, aiming also to challenge preconceptions of age through an examination of narrative fiction about old age. Woodward's crucial contributions to literary gerontology always inform this book, but my goals are different from hers.[10] I want to examine the explicitly textual (and in film's case physical) mechanisms that create elderly characters in prose and on film as exemplary of the ways in which attitudes toward old age, which circumscribe and culturally define the process of aging, are formed. My chief aim is to suggest that narrative fiction offers a vast potential for rethinking social problems, akin to that of critical theory but with broader appeal.

This analysis focuses largely on the Canadian context because I feel well positioned to witness the constant bombardment of images and descriptions within Canada. Further, a group of innovative narrative works of fiction and film published and released in Canada in the second half of the twentieth century address old age and offer audiences new vantage points. The selected narratives adapt key conventional narrative devices to their ends in order to play on and counter mainstream representations of aging. I by no means argue that narrative fiction *necessarily* has a particular or salutary social effect, nor do I suggest that fiction and film, especially the works studied here, are widely appreciated. Rather, I explore the imaginative potential of literary and film narratives and seek to claim that fictional narrative presents the *possibility* of profound social reconfiguration.

In the 1950s and 1960s Simone de Beauvoir and Margaret Laurence published fiction that takes on a relatively new subject matter: age, from the perspective of middle and old age. In the following chapter I explore a repertoire of attitudes toward aging through these works of fiction and examine the cultural construction of age that each enacts. Reading de Beauvoir's fiction through her critical treatise on age, *Old Age* (1970), allows a cross-fertilization that exposes the social construction of age in keeping with de Beauvoir's famous articulation of the construction of gender: Woman is made, not born. Laurence's nonagenarian protagonist, Hagar Shipley, constructs her own aging in keeping with stereotypical attitudes of disgust, horror, and physical unreliability. She attempts to evoke a past Hagar she desires through the present Hagar she fears terribly, and the resulting tension forces a discomforting distance through bathetic, bestial metaphors that describe a current self. The trope of mirror gazing pervades negative fiction of aging because characters struggle with a new self-identification in connection with a changed physical form. Both de Beauvoir and Laurence hint at the larger problem of social understandings of physical form, and the increasingly constructive depictions of aging discussed in the following chapters move away from the mirror to the reflection in younger people surrounding the aging characters.

With *The Stone Angel* as a touchstone, chapter 2 explores how Joan Barfoot's *Duet for Three* (1985) and Hiromi Goto's *Chorus of Mushrooms* (1994) depart from previous conventions of equating age with decrepitude at the same time as they theorize grandmotherhood as a possibly liberatory social role for old women (though grandmotherhood is not the exclusive province of the elderly). Grandmotherhood surely entails social scripts similar to that of motherhood, but we currently lack a discourse on the institution of grandmotherhood. To begin the process of developing such a discourse, this chapter presents a little-discussed literary trope wherein the intergenerational conflict so common to mother-daughter relationships frequently resolves across generations, at least in literature, so that grandmothers and granddaughters appear able to work together to battle cultural forces. *Duet for Three* and *Chorus of Mushrooms* risk positive ageism in their idealization of the grandmother role. At the same time, the novels invite readers to experience the potential for certain old women to play a significant, new role of grandmother that exceeds the limitations of positive ageism. Despite considerable intergenerational acrimony in each novel, neither Frances nor Murasaki (the granddaughters) cancels her grandmother, metaphorically or otherwise. Instead they continue the older women's personal, gendered struggles and, particularly in Murasaki's case, stories. Of course, any grandmother is also a mother, and these novels carefully situate elderly women in at times conflicting roles.

Hagar Shipley, in *The Stone Angel,* Aggie, in *Duet for Three,* and Naoe, in *Chorus of Mushrooms,* share more than just old age—they are all old women living with their offspring, and they are all threatened with a move to a nursing home. In chapter 3 I discuss how, as nursing homes are thought of as repositories for useless, old bodies, they become, conceptually, repositories for negative attitudes toward aging. The two most disturbing aspects of typical treatments of institutional care are the assumption that old people are all the same and the creation of emotional and physical dependence. Current gerontological nursing textbooks suggest that a direct, individualized engagement with each elderly resident, technically named "reality orientation," could go a long way to debunk such detrimental and even life-threatening assumptions. May Sarton's *As We Are Now* (1973) provides a figurative perspective on the potential for elderly inmates—an appropriate term perhaps with regard to the institution she depicts—to demolish damaging stereotypes attached to nursing homes through their association with all that is thought to be terrible about growing old. Arla, the caregiver in Edna Alford's *A Sleep Full of Dreams* (1981), is a cipher for readers both in her developing interpretive skills and in her ambivalence toward her aging charges. Tyler, in Shani Mootoo's *Cereus Blooms at Night* (1996), works so hard to piece together Mala Ramchandin's devastating story that readers are forced to understand, through his transvestite self, the intricate communication strategies required to bring together disparate social groups. These depictions of institutional care, more than commenting on the possibilities of such facilities to provide improved care, demonstrate the complicated process of forming attitudes toward the frail old and help to counter the impetus to think of age as either positive or negative. They provide examples of how narrative fiction can offer a perspective on the individuality of elderly residents that differs from clinical interaction.

Families and institutions present conventional options for old women who feel compelled to change their living situations. Growing out of the constructive relationships that can develop within an institution, friendship and collaboration among old women can present another, less conventional, late-life choice. Feminist literary critics have devoted some attention to female-female relationships, and they allow me, in chapter 4, to turn one last time to contemporary fiction for a conceptualization that eschews both young-old and mother-daughter binary paradigms. Joan Barfoot's *Charlotte and Claudia Keeping in Touch* (1994) sets up the possibilities for both commonality and complementarity to benefit female friends. Cynthia Scott's *Company of Strangers* (1990) provides, through semifiction, a model of female friendship and community that grapples with its own construction and transformation in which the viewer participates. The overt hybridity of the National Film Board production emphasizes the possibilities narrative fiction offers to both underlining and affecting constructions of age. It is not just that forming female-female friendships late in life could contribute solace and practical solutions to housing dilemmas; it is also that thinking of the value of connections among old women and imagining the help they can offer each other forces a recognition of late-life value and knowledge.

Chapter 1

The Mirror Has Two Faces: Simone de Beauvoir's and Margaret Laurence's Ambivalent Representations

Both Simone de Beauvoir (1908–1986) and Margaret Laurence (1926–1987) struggled with the prospects and realities of their own aging. Both were revolutionary women writers published internationally and criticized as much as praised for their innovations, primarily in novelistic subject matter. Continents apart, they joined in an increasing movement toward making women's lives at all stages viable plot material; they centered work on middle-aged characters and the supposedly mundane lives accompanying that stage of life. In doing so, de Beauvoir and Laurence confronted readers with issues of aging from the perspective of middle-aged and, in Laurence's case, also elderly narrators. In *From the Hearth to the Open Road: A Feminist Study of Aging in Contemporary Literature,* Barbara Frey Waxman isolates a new fictional genre: *Reifungsromane,* or fiction of ripening. Both de Beauvoir and Laurence write novels that, as Waxman has argued for Reifungsromane, prepare a readership for fiction about old age. However, because both invest in physical form and the horror that late-life physical change can evoke in readers, and perhaps because both possess a deep-seated fear of the "ravages" of age, de Beauvoir's and Laurence's depictions of aging damage as much as they help in initiating new, constructive cultural models of aging. Readers could expect aging characters to be the protagonists and even narrators of major literary works and could expect such characters to be completely engaging; however, readers are also invited to join in a disgust toward aging bodies that promotes social misconceptions of age as alienating decrepitude.

In provoking a horror about the aging female body, de Beauvoir and Laurence draw on another aspect Waxman highlights within Reifungsromane, the trope of mirror gazing and concomitant reflections of age that the aging characters perceive in those surrounding them. Speaking in the psychoanalytic terms a mirror motif invites, in *Aging and Its Discontents,* Kathleen Woodward describes what has been called the mirror stage of old age:

> The I or ego which is developed in the mirror stage of infancy is structured precisely to resist the anxiety of bodily fragmentation. In old age, with one's position reversed before the mirror, the ego finds it more difficult to maintain its defenses. The Lacanian ambivalence that has been felt all one's life before mirrors—the constant checking and comparing—is exacerbated to an almost intolerable point. (1991, 68)

Woodward's ensuing explanation of how the mirror stage of old age—and its unbearability— extends to other bodies, leads to some troubling questions:

> Strangeness, the uncanny, old age, decrepitude, death, fear, danger—all are linked together in this momentary drama of the mirror stage of old age. In the mirror stage of old age, the narcissistic impulse directs itself *against* the mirror image as it is embodied literally and figuratively in the faces and bodies—the images—of old people. If, then, the mirror stage of infancy initiates the imaginary, the mirror stage of old age may precipitate the loss of the imaginary. Where then would we be located? Outside the mirror? Caught between the double and the absent? (ibid., 69)

Woodward tells an important story of how relating to a mirror encapsulates the negative associations that attach to old age currently: as she lists them, "strangeness, the uncanny, old age, decrepitude, death, fear, danger."

Speaking of fiction, Waxman notes a split interiority that accompanies mirror scenes: "This mirror imaging of an elder often appears in *Reifungsromane* within similar 'shock-of- recognition' scenes that convey the tension between youthful mental outlook and aging physical appearance" (1990, 39–40). Older characters frequently look in the mirror expecting to find the younger manifestation about which they have been daydreaming and are shocked to find an old person's image staring back. Not surprisingly, I have found mirror gazing to be most prevalent in novels that harbor negative self-descriptions. In particular,

Simone de Beauvoir's Anne Dubreuilh and Margaret Laurence's Hagar Shipley struggle to reconcile themselves with the aging bodies they find reflected. Because accepting the label "old" would mean incorporating negative social constructions of aging, these characters, away from the mirror, imagine themselves to remain young and contained.

Later narratives, such as author Hiromi Goto's *Chorus of Mushrooms* (1994) and screenwriter/director Marlene Gorris's *Antonia's Line* (1995) move beyond the mirror. They thereby invest in a more integrated sense of an aging self that incorporates a "youthful mental outlook" within an elderly frame, defying the binary opposition of young and old and celebrating instead the continuum that Waxman proposes. As Constance Rooke puts it, speaking more generally, "each new novel that reveals the power of old age as a subject for fiction increases not only the possible audience for such fiction, but also the appeal of that subject for the writer's imagination" (1992, 242). Rather than being caught between the "double and the absent," which Woodward draws on André Green to gloss as "persecution and mourning," later authors exceed both and present elderly characters who are singularly present. Rather than "outside the mirror," they are perhaps beyond it. However, although the mirror motif is prevalent in what one hopes will soon be an outdated representation of aging bodies, it depicts a process that most women (and men) undergo in coming to terms with the cultural and personal meanings of age. Further, a wholly constructive view on aging could of course incorporate mirror gazing, rather than turning away from physical reflection.

Simone de Beauvoir and the Social Construction of Age

In her introduction to *Figuring Age,* Kathleen Woodward asks a question crucial to age studies: "[H]ow could Simone de Beauvoir's huge book on aging go unremarked?" (1999, xi). Stephen Katz, in *Disciplining Old Age: The Formation of Gerontological Knowledge,* offers an explanation for the lapse: "If one reads Beauvoir from a gerontologistical position, her unfamiliar mixing of philosophical, artistic, literary and autobiographical sources with sociological and economic ones puts her work outside of gerontology and perhaps dangerously close to exposing its borders" (1996, 108). In Woodward's own contribution to her edited volume, "Inventing Generational Models: Psychoanalysis, Feminism, Literature," she refers to the American translation of de Beauvoir's contribution as presenting a "moving model of imagining old age" (1999, 156). In that same section, however, she resists de Beauvoir's work on the basis that it assumes a young readership and supports two abhorrent assumptions: that being old is physically revolting and that the elderly are powerless economically. These are important problems in de Beauvoir's lengthy analysis that evokes an emotion dangerously akin to pity toward what de Beauvoir could have figured as a vibrant, powerful social group. However, her work is innovative both in taking on new subject matter and also in her manner of study. She pioneers a crucial research paradigm in her interdisciplinary study of old age, and in particular she explicitly and implicitly privileges literature throughout. It makes sense, then, to read her midlife fiction in light of her nonfiction prose about old age. The juxtaposition clarifies the strain evoked between a desire to understand old age and a desire not to be—or be thought of as—old.

In *Old Age* [*La vieillesse*], de Beauvoir eloquently articulates both the essence and the effect of her constructionist view (foreshadowed in *The Second Sex* [*Le deuxième sexe*]). In saying, "by the way in which a society behaves towards its old people it uncovers the naked, and often carefully hidden, truth about its real principles and aims," she claims that how a society views old age says more about the society than it does about old age (1977, 99). The imbrication of the social with the individual in de Beauvoir's writing makes particularly poignant the way in which a seeming terror of old age pervades virtually all of her work (with the exception perhaps of *Pour une morale de l'ambiguité* [*The Ethics of Ambiguity*]): her fiction, autobiographical works, and essays. As T. H. Adamowski states in his 1970 review of *Old Age:* "Since the appearance of *Le Deuxième Sexe,* in such works as *Les Mandarins, La Force des Choses,* and *Une Mort Très Douce,* her readers have seen Mme. De Beauvoir increasingly concerned with another 'destiny.' Now, in her latest work, *La Vieillesse,* she has kept a promise made in *La Force des Choses* and given us a work on a topic that some of her readers have considered to be her particular obsession" (1970, 394). De Beauvoir's obsession extends from her critical work into her construction of fictional characters. Since the *Second Sex* chapter "From Maturity to Old Age" was published in 1948, de Beauvoir has innovatively portrayed central fictional characters obsessed with their changing female bodies and explored her own and her mother's later life in autobiography. That she finds middle-aged women viable topics for fiction and that she chooses to "elevate her mother's drama and death to the role of a worthy literary subject" itself merits discussion (Kadish 1989, 636).[1] That she also makes old age and particularly its social construction and ramifications the topic of a book-length academic study confirms her status as an intellectual pioneer.

De Beauvoir's lesser-known book-length study of old age echoes and transforms the argument of her most popular treatise, *The Second Sex,* which famously argues that women are made, not born. *Old Age* makes the same argument for senescence, which she calls "not solely a biological, but also a cultural fact" (1977, 20). De Beauvoir's decision that old age merited her lengthy consideration makes her an innovator in cultural studies of the phenomenon that is only now beginning to garner serious and sizeable critical attention, and so her methodology acts as a model for current studies that attempt to follow her interdisciplinary example.[2] As with gender in *The Second Sex,* de Beauvoir defines old age as *otherness,* and her textual attempt to "break the conspiracy of silence" about old age, through anthropological, historical, medical, and literary analyses, evaluates various cultural milieux as constitutive of the experience that denigrates old age (8). De Beauvoir is among the first to claim that old age is created contextually and is not a purely biological and chronological phenomenon.[3]

De Beauvoir explicitly defends her decision to analyze literature in a study of old age. She turns to literary data to support her overall claim in the third chapter of *Old Age* through what she claims to be necessity, explaining that there is very little available information about old age at certain historical moments and that what little is available comes through the culturally determined form of literary creation. Implicitly, though, de Beauvoir turns to literary data throughout her treatise because she perceives that it offers distinct and important insights that enhance studies of old age. Her own evaluation of literary among other cultural artifacts to support numerous claims about age and society motivates the continued study of the contribution (potential and actual) of literary artifacts to studies and processes of aging.

When de Beauvoir sets out to explain the situation of "Old Age in Historical Societies," she explains that "written evidence" tends to categorize old people under the larger rubric of adult, but that "in mythology, in literature and in representative art" a picture of old age that "varies according to the century and to the place" emerges (99). When she continues her chronological study with an analysis of contemporary social norms, she claims that literature is no longer a necessary source: "Because of the mass of documentary evidence that we have on the present state of the aged, that provided by literature is only of minor interest; and in any case it does not amount to much" (237). She claims that she draws on literature only when other sources are not largely available and feels comfortable doing so because literary texts participate in the cultural context that she claims governs the construction of old age.

Although she continually refers to myth in her "Ethnological Data" chapter and continues to refer to literary texts in "Old Age in Present-Day Society" and even in Part II, de Beauvoir only overtly justifies her reliance on fiction as source in the earlier section "Old Age in Historical Societies." She feels able, in that chapter, to divine "the attitudes of historic societies towards old people and the relevant images that they have worked out for themselves" (240). She cautions that because the "poets" and "lawgivers," upon whom she frequently relies, come from privileged backgrounds, because "the picture [of old age they provide] is blurred, uncertain and contradictory," and because "they never say anything but part-truths and very often they lie" (99), she cannot rely on them to provide her a fully rounded perspective on the experience of aging. Accordingly, she necessitates interpretation as a strategy for teasing out the full or implied truths proffered by the "poets," who at least "are the more sincere, however, because they express themselves more spontaneously" (99–100). She admits that she does not offer a "general outline of the history of old age," but she does not otherwise apologize for relying solely on literary sources in her historical overview (240).

De Beauvoir's unabashed pairing of ethnographic and more traditionally historical data with literature juxtaposes sources that complement each other's analytical contributions to the extent that she can effectively demonstrate the culturally determined (that is, literally delineated by cultural artifacts) historical specificity of old age. An enormous range of literary texts following different Western European traditions, as well as one Chinese example, and genres from antiquity until the nineteenth century demonstrate the various interpretations, understandings, and valuations of old age historically. Hence she can claim to chart a progression of how Western and Chinese societies regard old age.

De Beauvoir exemplifies her methodology when she presents Renaissance literature's treatment of old age as evidence of how old people are not deemed worthy subjects of study and of how Renaissance English society usually dismissed them as unchangeably decrepit. De Beauvoir claims that during the Renaissance, "Literature, whether it glorified or disparaged old age, always buried it under a heap of preconceived ideas, hiding it instead of making it apparent" (183). She speculates, though not entirely convincingly, on Shakespeare's motivations for countering the prevailing tendency in Renaissance literature and instead situating tragic struggle within an aged male character in *King Lear:*

> Many people have asked what reasons Shakespeare can have had for writing *King Lear,* that is to say for incarnating humanity in an aged man. Perhaps he was moved to do so by the tragic lot of the aged in the English towns and countryside—the fate to which they had been reduced. When the manorial system broke down under the Tudors and unemployment played havoc in the towns, beggary spread everywhere, although—except under Edward VI—it was forbidden. It is not impossible that the wretchedness of these old, bewildered, penniless, destitute wanderers may have been the inspiration for the aged king. (187)

She offers historical data to support her literary interpretation in a manner typical of the way in which she amasses evidence for her claim that old age varies according to cultural constraints. She clearly merits literature as having a distinct and sizeable contribution both to the actual construction of the phenomenon she studies and to its study. She continually returns to literary endeavors, and she concerns herself not only with the reading of literature as source material but also with the type of literary production old people should attempt. For de Beauvoir, literature offers rich support to large, complicated, and controversial claims about an underdeveloped area of cultural understanding. As in the case of her decision to devote sustained interdisciplinary attention to the situation of women in *The Second Sex,* de Beauvoir's choice to unravel some problems and potentials of aging is groundbreaking and vital. In yet another anomalous study, de Beauvoir quietly and forcefully turns to anomalous sources.

Old Age itself is composed of many narratives: some de Beauvoir's, some literary, some scientific, and some descriptive. As Catherine Clément puts it in "Peelings of the Real," "*Old Age* is made of multiple stories. Stories by ethnographers, by historians, by philosophers: stories in any case, stories intertwined, marvellously told, small works of art in detailed writing" (1979, 170). One of de Beauvoir's greatest (and mostly overlooked) accomplishments is her ability (which Clément labels as art) to inhabit different discourses in order to explode them. Those who criticize her for favoring the masculine or scientific miss the impact of her technique of speaking deliberately and critically from within a problematic mode of expression. Linda Zerilli explains in reference to *The Second Sex:* "Beauvoir does not uncritically adopt but subversively inhabits the putatively impartial male voice that deduces the reproductive function of the woman from that of the female, the passivity of the female from that of the egg. Mimicking the language of reproductive biology, Beauvoir exposes a comic absurdity that signals a lack of scientific certitude" (1992, 118). By combining narrative modes, de Beauvoir reveals the inner assumptions of different ways of talking about age, so that no one narrative form can be authoritative. Literary narrative, to her mind, does not just provide cultural data but must also be carefully interpreted to tease out the constructive force it can have socially.

In *Old Age,* de Beauvoir combines the biological with the cultural to argue that the internal and external experiences of old age differ: "Yet our private, inward experience does not tell us the number of our years; no fresh perception comes into being to show us the decline of age. . . . Old age is more apparent to others than to the subject himself: it is a new state of biological equilibrium, and if the ageing individual adapts himself to it smoothly he does not notice the change" (1977,

316). The equilibrium implies a balance between external perceptions of physical changes and internal absorption of gradual changes that do not shock the self into recognizing aging. De Beauvoir claims that as a body inevitably enters into a period of biological decline, various cultural assumptions become ascribed to it regardless of whether its person acknowledges or even notices the physical changes: "In our society the elderly person is pointed out as such by custom, by the behaviour of others and by the vocabulary itself: he is required to take this reality upon himself" (324). The "fresh perception" of old age comes from internalizing cultural assumptions—usually ageism—resulting from people's visual interaction. This is why others can more easily perceive old age than the "subject himself." The self gradually adapts to the "inward" aspects of aging and can always perceive greater age in others. These inward experiences contrast the external dimension of late life that takes into account the appearance of physical change only. Others read those physical changes and react in such a way as to encourage the adoption of the established customs and particular vocabulary that accompany age culturally. De Beauvoir's argument that an understanding of old age directly affects (constructs) the perception of aging people tracks this progression from biological exteriority to mental interiority to cultural exteriority. Her own midlife fiction also tracks the process at the same time as it showcases the customs and vocabulary that surround age in mid-twentieth-century France.

In *Old Age,* de Beauvoir elucidates the exact role she conceives literature, and specifically fiction, of playing in depictions of old age, particularly in relation to the aging writer (perhaps because she herself shifted from writing fiction to solely autobiographical writing late in life). She initially differentiates the texts produced by nonfiction writers from those by fiction writers in terms of the type of data they offer to a study of old age:

> [I]t is important to realize that the expression "old age" has two very different meanings through the various pieces of evidence that we possess. It is either a certain social category which has greater or lesser value according to circumstances. Or for each person it is one particular fate: his own. The first point of view is that of the lawgivers and moralists; the second that of the poets; and for the most part they are radically opposed. (99)

She uses *poets* as an extremely general term mostly for the purpose of making a distinction as well as underlining the historical scope of her study that begins at a time when poetry was a central mode of literary expression. Having distinguished literature (produced by poets) as a distinct, individualized textual mode, she continues her content-based examination and further delineates genre boundaries, saying that the novel is "the least suitable form of literature for the elderly writer" (449). She argues that, within the literary realm that she has already configured as dedicated to and reliant on individual experience, "more than any other literary form, the novel requires that the present should be shattered in favour of an unreal world; and that world has life and colour only if it is rooted in very early fantasies. Daily happenings and the immediate world may provide the novelist with support or with a starting-point: but he has to transcend them, and he can only do so well by drawing from his own depths" (450). Rather than being better able to write fiction because of increased life experience, de Beauvoir argues that, because novels rely on imaginative extensions of inner convictions, elderly novelists risk simply repeating themselves. A novel must engage with readers' imaginations, and, in her disappointing view, an elderly writer is past imagining new possibilities.[4]

In her conclusion to *Old Age,* de Beauvoir blames the nature of culture for many problems the elderly face: "If culture were not a mere inactive mass of information, acquired once and for all and then forgotten, if it were effectual and living, and if it meant that the individual had a grasp upon his environment that would fulfil and renew itself as the years go by, then he would be an active, useful citizen at every age" (603). This claim could be read as a call for the type of fiction that Aritha Van Herk seeks in her "Desire in Fiction," when the contemporary Canadian author suggests that it is "time to abandon the rehearsed context for more challenging frontiers" (1992, 84). If cultural products presented ways of thinking through social problems, then an engagement with that culture could result in an improved late life. If fiction about old age challenged destructive attitudes toward age (as does Van Herk's *No Fixed Address* [1986]) rather than replicating troubling patterns, then old age itself could be an utterly different stage of life. And de Beauvoir's own reasons for excluding the elderly as potential authors of novels might dissipate.

Simone de Beauvoir's Midlife Fiction

In her own narrative fiction of aging, de Beauvoir does not offer a particularly constructive or challenging perspective, particularly of the physical aspects of growing old. Though clearly aware of the role that culture can play in transforming social attitudes toward age, de Beauvoir does not quite write the transformative fiction possible. Her works do, though, play the role Waxman suggests of preparing readers for the subject of aging—creating an audience who at least considers aging characters appropriate literary topics. What is more, she introduces that subject as complex and difficult to resolve even for strong female central characters who have otherwise exceeded standard restrictions to occupation and reductions to mere bodies. Although she never takes on extreme old age as a central literary topic, late life looms over her midlife fiction. Her works, especially *Les Mandarins* (1954) (*The Mandarins* [1957]), which is the focus of the following section, prepare and expand on theories, laid out philosophically in *Old Age,* that chart the progress of the self-recognition of age. *La femme rompue* (1968) (*The Woman Destroyed* [1969])—especially "The Age of Discretion," which is the only one of the three novellas I touch on here—and *Les belles images* (1966 [trans. 1968]) also participate in the process to some degree and deserve mention.

Current critical attention focuses mainly on de Beauvoir's memoirs and essays, but her fiction develops many of the same themes more fully and effectively, and, because she herself draws on fiction prolifically to prove her theses in both *The Second Sex* and *Old Age,* her own novels merit close scrutiny. Despite differences in genre and narrative technique, de Beauvoir's *Les Mandarins,* "The Age of Discretion," and *Les belles images* contain a common thread. Each narrative presents a middle-aged woman who, because of some interaction with a man in her life (son, husband, or new lover), becomes newly preoccupied with approaching old age. Elaine Marks claims that in "*Les Belles Images* (1966) and in the collection of novellas, *La Femme Rompue* (1967), the social and psychological problems associated with aging play a central role in the lives of the female protagonists" (1987, 184). In itself this does not seem remarkable, but compared to typical novel subject matter of young romance and masculine achievement, de Beauvoir's choice to foreground age deserves note. Perhaps she deliberately shows what comes after the happy ending of typical romance narratives. De Beauvoir does not expressly play with novelistic expectation to the same extent as the more recent novels I discuss, but she does foreground their innovation by subverting the expected passivity and domesticity of the subject matter. Furthermore, she centers psychological plots on middle-aged women who feel and act on intense physical desire (female physical desire presents a unique and rare topic for even contemporary fiction) even though they lament the loss of youth because they perceive their age to eliminate them as the object of sexual desire.

The combined rejections of Anne Dubreuilh by Lewis Brogan and Paula Mareuil by Henri Perron in *Les Mandarins,* as well as the caricature of Lucie Belhomme's middle-aged supposed lack of charms, do not exactly add up to what Margaret Morganroth Gullette has named the midlife women's progress novel, "a splendid new liberatory genre" that she claims emerged in the late twentieth century. Those novels make "change and choice and enlightenment seem accessible *via*—not in spite of—aging" (1997, 90). Such literary works could very well be said to counter the stasis pervading cultural notions of middle age. De Beauvoir's own grappling with middle and old age stops short of such a challenge: Most constructive developments come "in spite of" and not "via" the aging that physical change signals. Nonetheless, her midlife fiction subtly presents previously and continually underrepresented subject positions (particularly those of middle-aged women) so that it offers readers opportunities to engage anew with unfamiliar perspectives. Accordingly, her novels lay the groundwork for more "progressive" novels simply by making middle-aged women the objects and subjects of sexual desire and eschewing (sometimes from within) conventions of youthful literary sex in *Les Mandarins.*

Participating in cultural assumptions of decrepitude, Anne Dubreuilh initially considers her first sexual experience in the novel unseemly; although she is only thirty-nine years old, "to think of myself naked in his arms was as incongruous as imagining him embracing my old mother" (1960, 96). Dubreuilh displaces her aging onto what she perceives to be a more appropriate vehicle—her mother's body. The implications for women's sexuality inherent in this displacement are discouraging and underline how de Beauvoir, in her early forties at the time, plays on the displacement along an age continuum mentioned in Mary Russo's "The Scandal of Anachronism." Scriassine's persistent desire convinces Dubreuilh of her own desirability, but she can find that credible only if it means she is not old: "His impatience seemed to assure me that, after all, I wasn't my old mother. Since he desired me, I was forced to believe I was desirable, if only for an hour" (96). There is no possibility, still, for Dubreuilh to revise her misunderstanding of her mother's sexuality to reckon with her new experience. Because Dubreuilh, as is typical, associates sex with youth, the sexual act compels her to evaluate how her body defies conventions of youthful body: "He threw off the sheet, and at the same moment it occurred to me that the room was poorly heated and that I no longer had the belly of a young girl. The mutilated flower burst suddenly into bloom, and lost its petals" (98). The desiccation of an already clichéd figure for young female beauty conveys how Dubrueilh thinks about her own experience through existing understandings about sexuality. She recognizes how that experience does not match circulating cultural narratives, and de Beauvoir explodes a clichéd metaphor for romance. The entire experience leads Dubreuilh (at thirty-nine) to resign herself to the approach of old age: "Old age is awaiting me; there's no escaping it. Even now I can see its beginnings in the depths of the mirror. . . . But there's no way in the world to halt the infirmities of age" (103). Not only does the contrast she perceives between her nearly middle-aged body and her past youthful body make her seek old age mentally, it also brings on a harmful association between old age and illness. The connection is devastatingly negative—Dubreuilh's sexual experience, because she feels she is no longer young (and there is not the same attention to Scriassine's advancing age), makes her think not only of a "loss" of beauty but also of an impending "loss" of health. Dubreuilh embraces negative understandings of old age as she witnesses the emergence within the mirror of the other that she perceives will be her elderly self.

Dubreuilh's subsequent obsession with the young American Lewis Brogan nearly robs her of her earlier resolve to "keep going" (103), the only solution she had been able to find to the damaging confrontation with old age invoked by her sexual encounter with Scriassine. Her first encounter with the younger Brogan makes her compare herself to younger women in terms of appearance: "What, after all, did he and I have in common? The women seated opposite him were young and pretty. Did they please him? I realized that there must certainly have been young, pretty women in his life" (420). The realization signifies her belief that Brogan could not possibly choose to be with an older body—her self-perception of sexual attractiveness has hinged upon her belief that she must be the youngest, and therefore most desirable, woman he knows. As with her interaction with Scriassine, her contact with Brogan makes her further aware of encroaching old age: "Lewis remained as far from me as ever, but each day brought me closer to old age" (526). She compares Brogan and herself in terms of age, finding that she comes up short; she also compares what she perceives to be an appropriate sexual object (a young female body) with how she thinks of her own body (past beauty), finding once more that she comes up short. The chasms she senses once again reinforce for her the approach of old age.

On renewed contact with Brogan, in the same way Scriassine's desire made her at least acknowledge her own desirability, Dubreuilh manages momentarily to reconcile her aging body with Brogan's passion: "With my frayed life, my skin no longer brand-new, I was creating happiness for the man I loved" (559). Momentarily, she accepts her sexuality alongside her increasing age. Despite this brief invigoration, she cannot, because of her age, fathom changing her life: "But at my age, you can't throw your whole life overboard; it's too late. We met each other too late" (574). She simply wishes for a few years of sexual happiness: "That was all I wanted—a few years. I was too old for pledges of eternal love" (594). Disturbingly and perhaps deliberately, the encounters between Dubreuilh and these two male characters initially reduce aging to an examination of how women appear to men and to themselves as sexual objects. If woman is equal to flesh, then age means certain doom.

Having left Brogan after their second encounter, invigorated by the validation of his desire for her, Dubreuilh indulges in feelings of youthfulness, turning once again to the mirror: "Freshened by a new coat of make-up, my reflection in the mirror was satisfying. 'No, six months from now, I shan't have aged much; I'll see Lewis again and he'll still love me.' and when I entered Claudie's salon, I wasn't far from thinking, 'After all, I'm still young!'" (665) Gone, momentarily, are her feelings of incongruity, but only because she feels momentary youth that cosmetics help her to simulate and not because she accepts that her middle-aged body is actually sexy. Separated from Brogan's physical desire, she reckons with an imagined decrepitude that quickly dissolves her mask of youth, and she tries once more to reconcile how she perceives her current physical condition with her renewed physical passion: "That little spark of youth which had dazzled me for a moment fizzled out all too quickly. Glass mirrors are too indulgent; the faces of these women of my own age, that flabby skin, those blurred features, those drooping mouths, those bodies so obviously bulging under their corsets—these were the true mirrors. 'They're old, worn-out hags,' I thought, 'And I'm the same age as they'" (666–67). As de Beauvoir outlines the process of internalized ageism in *Old Age,* Dubreuilh encounters the physical appearance of her age, engages with that mentally, and adheres to its cultural meaning. Unable to reconcile what she considers to be realistic middle age with sexual passion, Dubreuilh once again tries to resign herself to what she perceives as inevitably approaching old age, this time explaining her reasons for doing so: "I hasten to tell myself, 'I'm finished, I'm old.' In that way, I cancel out those thirty or forty years when I will live, old and finished, grieving over a lost past; I'll be deprived of nothing since I've already renounced everything. There's more caution than pride in my sternness, and fundamentally it covers up a huge lie: by rejecting the compromises of old age, I deny its very existence" (669). Dubreuilh defends herself against what she perceives to be the bleak period of old age by reaching for the end point early. By hurrying to embrace the decrepitude she associates with aging, Dubreuilh relieves herself of the responsibilities associated with youthful passion, rejects the process of growing old in favor of what she perceives as the product, and accordingly sabotages her love relationship.

Indeed, Dubreuilh's next encounter with Brogan is devastating and seals her abrupt, premature acceptance of old age. She subsequently contemplates a suicide that she cannot carry out because of consideration for her daughter and her daughter's expectations of her with relation to her granddaughter: "I can't impose my corpse and everything that would come after that on their hearts" (761). Despite an internal and somewhat forced acceptance of encroaching old age, she chooses not to avoid it via suicide because of a social, in particular familial, role. Nonetheless, as Yolanda Patterson points out in "Simone de Beauvoir and the Demystification of Motherhood," "In her newborn granddaughter she sees the inevitability of her own decline and demise, of the oblivion which eventually awaits us all" (1986, 101). Reading old age into the features of an infant emphasizes the disproportionate reaction Dubreuilh has to her own eventual "demise": "On her inscrutable little face I again see my death. One day she'll be as old as I am, and I'll no longer be here" (de Beauvoir 1957, 759). Rather than transferring lost hopes onto a removed generation (as some later Canadian novels do), Dubreuilh recognizes the equal inevitability of her granddaughter Maria's eventual decline, nearly kills herself because of the futility of existence it implies, and yet ultimately chooses not to because of her responsibility to that grandchild.

Whereas Dubreuilh submits to familial—and particularly maternal—responsibilities, her friend Paula Mareuil martyrs herself solely out of romantic love. In a stubborn attempt to deny the futility of continuing to live for Perron, Mareuil refuses to acknowledge the passage of time: "There's a Rimbaud, a Baudelaire, a Stendhal [un Rimbaud, un Baudelaire, un Stendhal]. They were older, younger, but their whole lives are contained in a single picture. There's only one Henri, and I shall always be I. Time is powerless to change it; it's we who betray ourselves, not time" (239). Her refusal to acknowledge the passage of time reflects her desperate attempt to cling to the time when her relationship with Perron was viable and to refuse to acknowledge its development and decline. Mareuil's reaction, although necessarily implicit, resembles Dubreuilh's explicit resigned acceptance of approaching old age in that both are motivated by a desire/need to preserve domestic sanctity. Accordingly, aside from Mareuil's futile attempts to negate the inevitable changes time has wrought, de Beauvoir represents her aging only from without, and so necessarily outside the domestic sphere she has to protect. Because she carefully guards her domestic space—it contains only Perron and herself—no new changed vantage points of her late life can violate it from within.

In both *Old Age* and her fiction, de Beauvoir presents a strict division between the interiority and the exteriority of aging. De Beauvoir claims, in *Old Age,* "since it is the Other within us who is old, it is natural that the revelation of our age should come to us from outside— from others" (320).[5] Whereas Dubreuilh fails to acknowledge her own physical change despite her internal acceptance, "and as for me, I hadn't aged, I wasn't disfigured" (702), Perron reads her internal struggles as physical change: "Anne had aged markedly" (722). Similarly, Mareuil's denial of the passage of time stands in stark contrast to Dubreuilh's brutal acceptance of it, particularly when Dubreuilh points it out to her: "'You're confusing things,' I said. 'When you're seventy you'll still be you, but you'll have a different relationship with people, with things.' I paused briefly and added. 'With your mirror'" (239). Evoking her own perceptions of "the depths of the mirror" (103), Dubreuilh directly confronts Mareuil's entire motivation for refusing to acknowledge her own aging. Dubreuilh has perhaps too large a stake in making Mareuil accept the changes that come with time because Mareuil's acknowledgement will justify Dubreuilh's fatalism. Disturbingly, this exchange hinges entirely on the interpretation of physical changes, once again evoking (or provoking) de Beauvoir's tracking of the internalization and subsequent externalization of age identity.

Speaking of Mareuil's changing physical appearance, Dubreuilh tells readers, "Instead of artfully engraving itself, time had brutally marked that noble, baroque mask which still well deserved admiration, but which would have been more in place in a museum than a salon" (451). She honors Mareuil's defiance of time by placing her metaphorically within an institution that houses static artifacts appraised to have value because they signify a past time. However, Dubreuilh submits to the ultimate power of time and, after Mareuil has been publicly exposed as an old woman, reevaluates her physical state: "Paula had been so beautiful that it never occurred to me she could one day cease completely to be so—there was something in her face that would resist everything. And suddenly, you could see: like everyone else's, it was made of spongy flesh—more than eighty per cent water" (536). Age plays the ultimate equalizer here so that whatever distinguished Mareuil earlier now dissolves into her physical state, which becomes her entire identity as an aging person. Beauty was a distinguishing marker for Mareuil, and Dubreuilh perceives age as taking that distinction from her. The physical changes Dubreuilh reads in Mareuil's face and Dubreuilh's interpretation of them diminish physical individuality in the manner of many current theories of aging. De Beauvoir has Dubreuilh once again present age as the loss of youth, signaled by desirability to men. A disturbing connection continues from that signification: acceding to negative cultural notions not just of aging, but also of femininity. Such notions value women only in relation to men and condemn late life as a time of physical decline that changes potential relationships between women and men. The most optimistic reading of this depiction is that de Beauvoir, by offering readers Dubreuilh's culturally sanctioned perspective on Mareuil's physical form, allows them access to a new understanding of how particular social notions about aging and physical change can damage. A more negative reading interprets de Beauvoir as buying into cultural understandings of age as loss of femininity and being able to present age only as decay.

Mareuil's own interpretation, or lack thereof, of her physical frame complicates the tension between possible readings of age in *Les Mandarins.* Mareuil's rigid denial of her aging is markedly thwarted by Perron's new lover, who, not knowing of Mareuil's claim to Perron, sees and describes Mareuil as a "fat old woman" (487). Readers have followed Dubreuilh and Perron's narration, both of which focus on Paula's beauty. Indeed, Mareuil's value to Perron had entirely been her exquisite beauty and as Perron's love for her subsides, so too does that beauty seem to. Either Mareuil's youth faded and Perron's desire (masquerading as love) faded in return, or Perron's desire (sincerely channeled into love) diminished, leaving Mareuil undesired and therefore figured by others as aging. In either case, Mareuil is unaware of the shift. Her refusal to acknowledge the passage of time (which coincides with her refusal to admit to Perron's disenchantment) may serve her well internally, but she cannot prevent others from perceiving (or constructing) her physical transformation. Indeed, she refuses to face the changes others perceive as wrought by time, and that refusal eventually results in paranoid delusion. In de Beauvoir's literary world (in contrast to contemporary North American culture), ignoring age signals pathology. Mareuil is "cured" of her refusal of time only after undergoing therapy. However, an appropriate investment in social relationships means accepting age, often before its arrival, because forging relationships and examining attitudes, reactions, and physical transformations of others forces an acknowledgement of age. Dubreuilh preempts a social reaction by taking on the meaning of age as soon as possible.

De Beauvoir does not provide readers of *Les Mandarins* with an appropriate touchstone attitude toward aging, unless perhaps that is the role she expects Dubreuilh to play. *Les Mandarins* is not an especially liberatory novel for women and especially not for aging women. An engagement with Dubreuilh and Mareuil, however, at least provides readers a new vantage point, however devastating, in relation to the gender specificity of age. Because of the troubling construction of female value, age becomes an especially poignant female concern. Readers must sympathize with, or be disgusted by, Dubreuilh's fatalistic acceptance of her perceived failure as a sexual being. The narrative structure, alternating between Dubreuilh's and Perron's voices, places the age plot into a larger context. Dubreuilh's is only one narrative voice in the novel, which alternates between two major plots and narrations. Because readers see Dubreuilh from within—through her narration—and from without—through Perron's narration—they can better understand that cultural constructions of aging can be completely damaging and debilitating, as much as any actual physical change. The male political plot (which explores the question of an intellectual's personal commitment), juxtaposed with the female aging plot (which explores questions of how women age and handle aging), forms a complex address to the reader, who is left to recompose perspectives on both dilemmas, political and personal. The combination may also reflect de Beauvoir's own battles with self-perception and her relationship with Sartre, who had taken on an intense love affair with Dolorès Vanetti Ehrenreich not long before de Beauvoir drafted *Les Mandarins.* As Kate and Edward Fullbrook explain, "The initial stages of Sartre's liaison with Dolorès seemed to have impaired his ability to work" (1994, 163). Intensifying the characterization of Perron (who may in part reflect Sartre) as obsessed with his political work diminishes the importance of his love life. Within the novel, from the perspective of Dubreuilh's suicidal personal anguish, Perron's political agitation seems overdone, and from the perspective of Perron's lofty political goals,[6] Dubreuilh's self-absorbed struggle with her aging body seems minute. Each plot is treated out of proportion within the confines of the novel, and each plot line reveals the other to be overblown.

De Beauvoir's ambivalence toward aging, as encompassed by the dual voices in *Les Mandarins,* emerges through a single perspective in her short story "Age of Discretion," which is part of the collection titled *La femme rompue.* The three novellas, "The Age of Discretion," "Monologue," and "The Woman Destroyed," work well together precisely because of a subversive thematic unity with respect to approaching old age and changing female social roles. Each central character displays disappointment in offspring and a need to seek fulfillment elsewhere, in marriage, in work, in insanity, and ultimately in the coming of age.

The protagonist of "Age of Discretion" accepts that she has, in her eyes, failed to bring up her son as she would have liked and resignedly renews her commitment to her aging husband and former pupils. Her recognition of the old people around her, especially her husband, changes, and so too does her relationship with new groups of pupils, to whom she compares her own age. These changes enable her to accept her own aging: "In earlier days I never used to worry about old people: I looked upon them as the dead whose legs still kept moving. Now I see them—men and women: only a little older than myself" (1969b, 10). Faced with a more or less static manifestation of age in the form of students (who appear in age cohorts year after year), she accepts the relationality of age implied by the "old people" around her. By reading the signs of aging on their bodies as similar to those on her own, she reinterprets age. Now the "old people" she sees are individuals rather than symbols of impending death.

The main character, who is never named, resents the perceived need to maintain a youthful approach and the implication that surrendering youth means surrendering in a larger sense: "Remaining young means retaining lively energy, cheerfulness and vitality of mind. So the fate of old age is the dull daily round, gloom and dotage. I am not young: I am well preserved, which is quite different. Well preserved; and maybe finished and done with" (60). External illusions of youth do not necessarily entail the exhausting energy of youth. The central character of "Age of Discretion" grapples with her fears of old age as ruin (as figured in the bodies of her husband and mother-in-law) and the gradual acceptance of the death of those around her in order to come to terms with her own "demise": "What nonsense, this intoxicating notion of progress, or upward movement, that I had cherished, for now the moment of collapse was at hand! It had already begun. And now it would be very fast and very slow: we were going to turn into really old people" (70). Though she recognizes that the "old people" around her are individuals, she has not erased their connection with impending death, and in acknowledging her own age, she confronts her own mortality. As in the case of Anne Dubreuilh, this character is defeated by an eagerness to embrace especially the negative facets of late life, without a strong sense of future possibilities: "Would the dread of ageing take hold of me again? Do not look too far ahead. Ahead there were the horror of death and farewells: it was false teeth, sciatica, infirmity, intellectual barrenness, loneliness in a strange world that we would no longer understand and that would carry on without us" (82). The phrase "intellectual barrenness" is particularly striking in view of de Beauvoir's own much-remarked-upon lifelong learning and teaching. In identifying herself as old, the central character contemplates the varied ailments she associates with aging.

De Beauvoir argues that women who rely most heavily on their "femininity" are those affected most by the external transformation that accompanies age, and by doing so she complicates the frequently discussed double bind of aging women face. In *Old Age,* she describes certain women who are thereby more reluctant to accept the other into whom aging turns them:

> There is nothing that obliges us in our hearts to recognize ourselves in the frightening image that others provide us with. That is why it is possible to reject that image verbally and to refuse it by means of our behaviour, the refusal itself being a form of assumption. This is a usual choice with some women who have staked everything on their femininity and for whom age means being entirely out of the running. They try to deceive the rest of the world by means of their

> clothes, make-up and behaviour; but above all they make a hysterical attempt at convincing themselves that they are not affected by the universal law. (328)

Femininity here seems to mean quite simplistically participating in cultural rituals that mark gender difference. De Beauvoir sensibly argues that women who construct self-worth on the basis of their appearance will mask their age in order to deny its effect on the foundation of how they construct their own value.

Dominique of de Beauvoir's *Les belles images* aptly represents a woman who has staked much on the external trappings of femininity. The initial description of Dominique is of someone who could be mistaken for thirty although she is in fact fifty-one years old. Throughout the novel she gradually accepts (albeit to a very small degree) that she is growing older, saying to her daughter, "'I can't believe that one day I'll be seventy'" (1969a, 14) and pointing out the signs on her neck and face. As she later weeps, Laurence (her daughter) realizes: "There was a flesh and blood woman with a heart under all those disguises, a woman who felt age coming on and who was terrified by loneliness: she [Dominique] whispered 'A woman without a man is a woman entirely alone'" (97). Dominique reconciles herself to her age by finding acceptable social roles to play: "Dominique was very much 'family party,' she was dressed in the character of 'youthful grandmother' in a discreet honey-coloured jersey dress, her hair nearer white than blonde" (119). She also settles on a suitable solution for her social plight: "'A married couple who come together again after a long separation so as to face old age together—people may be surprised, but they won't snigger'" (149). In order not to be a woman entirely alone, she reacts to her age by adapting to the only socially sanctioned option of companionship available to her. Even Dominique's interior struggles with aging concern themselves with maintaining an external persona that can be socially acceptable and old simultaneously. Once clothes and makeup can no longer mask her age, Dominique changes her behavior to match others' changing perceptions of her.

De Beauvoir does not portray extreme old age as central in any of her fiction. She is mostly preoccupied with middle-aged women who are obsessively aware of the approach of old age. Nonetheless, this is innovative subject matter that lays substantial groundwork both for later fiction about middle age and for the logical extension to fiction that foregrounds old age. De Beauvoir does not provide her protagonists with multiple liberatory possibilities, nor does she sugarcoat the devastating effects of physical change on women who are in fact relatively young. She does, however, fictionally address the problem of self-perceived deterioration and its particular effect on women whose projects, as her existentialist credo would put it, necessarily differ from those of men and are often more tied to physical beauty. Because of her focus on physical change, she participates in a convention of negativity about aging so that even her midlife fiction exudes a terror of old age that, though revealed to be out of proportion, could easily strike a chord with readers already anxious about what late life will bring. Still, in presenting fiction from the perspective of aging heroines and not shying away from physicality and even sexuality, she defies conventions that dictate suitable narrative material. Aging characters do not occupy only the margins of this fiction; though they do not really tell the new stories of aging I seek, they and their concerns about aging pervade the narratives to an extent that, at the very least, the need for new stories emerges.

Margaret Laurence's Figurative Evasions

Similar to de Beauvoir's, Margaret Laurence's contribution to age studies complicates as much as it clarifies. Laurence's personal ambivalence toward old age becomes especially poignant in the juxtaposition of her biography with the great critical acclaim her novel about old age received. Though she herself committed suicide rather than become like the character she had created, that character, the indomitable Hagar Shipley, shaped Laurence's literary career and contributed greatly to a continually growing literature of old age, especially in Canada. Hagar Shipley's intimate struggle with her aging body and commensurate self-hatred defies her literary legacy. When I presented a paper on *The Stone Angel* (1964) to a group of elderly people, one woman praised Hagar as an example of an elderly character with dignity. That this is her lasting impression is notable because Laurence depicts her as continually humiliated, especially by her tendency to belch and fart at inopportune moments. It is possible that Hagar's dignified legacy hails from a contemporaneous lack of articulate elderly women in literature, but it could also be precisely her struggle with physical ignominy that renders her dignified. *The Stone Angel* sets up the field of literary gerontology, especially that focused on women, precisely because of its vexatious tension between advocacy for the elderly and denigration of old age.

The Stone Angel was immediately published internationally, in Canada, the United States, and Britain, and has since attracted international critical attention to the extent that the American-published *New Perspectives on Margaret Laurence* has to state explicitly with some surprise (humorous to a Canadian reader) that studies of Laurence's work have been published elsewhere: "Several books on Margaret Laurence's writing (by

Canadians and a Scot) are published outside of America" (Coger 1996, xix). Laurence's choice of a female nonagenarian protagonist confronted contemporaneous literary standards and readers' expectations to the extent that she questioned her own sanity: "No seductions. No rapes. No murders. . . . It is the work of a lunatic, I think. It has hardly anything to recommend it to the general public" (quoted in King 1997, ix–xx). Poking fun, perhaps, at the melodrama required to make other fiction engaging, Laurence plays on the conventional expectations of readers in her anxiety. An old protagonist is thought to be past the suitable time for seduction, rape, and murder. Still, Laurence offers readers a remarkably compelling character who occupies a subject position not often considered interesting generally, let alone artistically. In doing so she has created possibilities for later female writers to project similar alternate realities and thereby further her ends of examining the possibilities for female independence and power fascinatingly situated in her grandfather's generation (Taylor 1996, 162).

In response to the likelihood of becoming simultaneously ill and old, suffering from the very cancer she had imagined for Hagar, Margaret Laurence herself chose suicide, writing in her journal, "I would rather let go now, then [*sic*] go on to be one of those old old [*sic*] ladies in the hospital. I don't want to be Hagar" (quoted in King 382). She felt she could not "bear all the storms of the humiliated & painful flesh" (ibid., 286). Laurence's biography devastatingly contradicts and yet reinforces the fictional narrative she had presented two decades earlier in *The Stone Angel*. Ironically, though, the possibilities harbored within that earlier construction of a difficult late life continue a potent connection with readers committed to countering the ageism that, in effect, killed Laurence. Aritha Van Herk explains the strength of Laurence's portrayal when she declares:

> I want to celebrate Margaret Laurence, who gave us *The Stone Angel* and Hagar Shipley, that proud and enduring grandmother who taught us what old age means and about the indignities of a faltering body, who represents backbone and courage. I want to celebrate the writer who created an old and sick and recalcitrantly dying woman and who teaches us to celebrate her too, just as all her books teach us to celebrate the grief and joy of a woman's life. (1992, 237)

When threatened with cancer, Laurence did not go so far as to celebrate or even continue her own late life. However, she writes such audacity into Hagar while treating her as an entire human being, only one of whose traits is old age, that readers stand to learn from her depiction.

I do not argue for a straightforward didacticism in my claims that novels may be able to alter social configurations. However, a strain within *Stone Angel* criticism implies that Hagar's depiction operates pedagogically. Van Herk refers to what the novel can "teach us." Clara Thomas provides backhanded praise for Laurence's creation when she says, "It is no compliment to a novel as a work of art to say that it might well be used as a textbook in geriatrics; or that its last pages are a perfect casebook on both the sad reassurances and the maddening frustrations of a patient in hospital" (1976, 74). Thomas implies that Laurence's account of old age is so convincing that it can provide new ways of thinking about aspects of late life. Though similarly negative about old age, Sara Maitland reinforces this reading of Laurence's apparent accuracy: "I do not know, anywhere in literature, a more convincing or moving account of old age; of the anger and fear and the humiliation, coupled with a completely unsentimental recognition of the manipulation and the craziness and meanness of a dangerous old woman" (1987, 44). It is not so much that Hagar Shipley exemplifies female late life but that her depiction affects readers emotionally and mentally, engaging them anew, unfortunately primarily with the physical vicissitudes of age. Laurence's novel offers a startling new perspective on old age, seemingly as faithful as it is unique, so that Thomas's double-edged praise should be taken seriously. Regardless of whether she faithfully portrays old age, which always remained outside her experience, Laurence's accomplishment in the gritty construction of Hagar Shipley presents a devastating challenge and circuitous pathway to committed readers.

Curiously, a critical tendency to ignore, underplay, or denigrate Hagar's age replicates the kinds of evasions Laurence situates in Hagar's own discourse about her aging body. Certain moments in *The Stone Angel* dominate criticism of the novel to the extent that a separate critical version emerges. Notably, most of the frequently chosen passages relate to Hagar and motherhood. Almost all of the articles discuss the opening of the novel in great detail, linking Hagar to the statue erected for her mother's grave. Also, most of the studies devote a considerable passage to the moment at which Hagar refuses to impersonate her mother by wearing a shawl at her brother's deathbed. Perhaps these continual overlapping references influence critical readings of the novel and lead to the frequent avoidance of age as a lens through which to examine the novel. As a result, because many critics avoid the troubling present-tense narrative featuring the indomitable Hagar daunted by age, few refer to the Silverthreads nursing home visit even though it is the central conflict of the novel's frame.

Because *Stone Angel* critics so often elide Hagar Shipley's old age with other concerns, accounts rarely capture the structure of the novel. Although the entire novel's narration by nonagenarian Hagar should make it impossible to consider *The Stone Angel* through any conduit but that of extreme old age, studies typically shy away from adopting or even admitting that subject position. Instead, the general impetus recently is to attempt to unify the novel from some other paradigmatic angle: theme, genre, or political status. Doing so encourages a recapitulation of Hagar Shipley's biography in a way that forgets how Laurence offers the entire fabula from the perspective of a particular, extremely old woman.

Many studies find coherence in the novel because of its biblical or literary imagery, because of its status as a confessional novel, or because of its impact as a feminist novel. *The Stone Angel* is coherent from all of these perspectives and many others, but the most obvious and necessary way to examine that coherence is via old age, as Constance Rooke, Barbara Frey Waxman, and Stephanie Demetrakopoulos have done. Laurence herself points out that the very structure of the novel, which provides critics the biographical recap they examine, deliberately mirrors the mental processes of the very old: "In a sense, I think this method ["present tense, with flashbacks in the past tense"] works not too badly in *The Stone Angel* simply because Hagar *is* so old, *is* living largely in her past, does—like so many old people— remember the distant past better than the present" (quoted in Thomas 1976, 66). Laurence explains why readers of all ages are able to consider her portrait of Hagar faithful—the controlled rambling of the narration matches cultural understandings of elderly thought patterns. Oddly, despite the deliberate and successful seemingly doddering narration, few studies of *The Stone Angel* directly address the extent to which old age governs the novel that thereby comments on the process of aging. Critics usually acknowledge Hagar's old age only in order to describe the "crazy," "mean," "dangerous," "churlish," "screeching," "outrageous" old woman (Maitland 1987, 44; Baum 1996, 157) in connection with her physical decline: "At ninety, when the book begins, she is grotesque with the fat ugliness of her old age" (Thomas 1976, 61).

Certain feminist approaches do consider Hagar's old age as part of a larger study of the novel, and, as a result, these studies discuss the novel's narrative configuration. Constance Rooke notes, in support of the narrative structure of the novel, that "we are made to sense the physically decrepit Hagar as a mask behind which the true Hagar continues to reside" (1982, 26). Rooke not only acknowledges both the narrative situation of the novel and its connection to late-life experience but also replicates the difficulties Hagar herself has with accepting her aging frame. Barbara Frey Waxman applies her term Reifungsroman to *The*

Stone Angel because the novel contains "the alienating effect of anger" (1990, 159), "the fall" as "common event of *Reifungsromane*" (160), the mirror (164), "remembrance of sex past" (168), confessional narrative (175), and an "emphasis . . . on the physical body and illness" (178). Waxman's consideration of Hagar's gender in connection with her age allows her to pinpoint the narrative structure of the novel and its potential effect on readers. In doing so, she recognizes the danger of a strict binary opposition between youth and age because of how it guides the painful confrontations in the novel. Stephanie Demetrakopoulos distinguishes Laurence's depiction of an old woman from characteristic male depictions in which "older women have often been seen as revoltingly lecherous, spending their days and nights plotting how sexually to entrap various men" (1982, 51). Demetrakopoulos directly contrasts Laurence's Hagar with Chaucer's Wyf of Bath and Joyce Cary's Sarah Monday, instead associating Hagar with a series of old women and female-constructed elderly female characters such as Lillian Hellman, May Sarton's Hilary Stevens, Tillie Olsen's protagonist in "Tell Me a Riddle," and Mary Daly's self-proclaimed Crone (52). Such readings provide a balanced view of the present and past narratives that make up *The Stone Angel,* thereby allowing for an interpretation of how youth transforms into age and emphasizing how the traits in Hagar that one could dismiss as typical of old women—stubbornness, alienation, bodily discomfort—in fact dominate her entire life story, from youth to old age.

My analysis concentrates on the effect that an aging narrator has on linguistic expression, and so it includes and even prioritizes a close reading of the present-tense narrative rather than focusing on the favorite retrospective moments of past studies. The supposed vicissitudes of late life and the gradual reckoning with the changes time has wrought imbue each scene (past and present) of the novel with surprising disclosures about late life that readers have to negotiate constantly. To my mind, Hagar's youth can be read only through age so that the two stand in contrast, but even more so in concert. Hagar's struggle to express herself comes across as emblematic of the losses of control that can come with age, and through her gaps in expression, readers capture the tensions faced by a character struggling with the social interpretations of age inflicted upon her.

Laurence presents an elderly narrator who tries to manipulate socially constructed images of the elderly. Hagar Shipley encounters her present plight through reminiscences that explore past and underline present attempts at physical and social escape. The narration leaves readers privy only to her particular and unreliable perspectives on both her physical present and her past. All of the information approaches readers via an especially focused and filtered lens. Hagar's retelling consists of self-evaluation based on fear of judgment of others and her own physical transformation. She appears unable to grapple with both perceived failure in each person from her past and incomprehensible physical unreliability. She distances her narration from herself (and by extension from the reader) through metaphor. Readers do not have to gaze directly at her aged flesh (and the lacks and absences it represents) but rather reach an understanding by means of varied fetid vehicles. Those vehicles operate as a mask, so that Hagar designs her metaphors to make almost literally visible the negative assumptions about old age and hide its potential beyond that negativity.[7]

Repeated mirror-gazing scenes poignantly underscore Hagar Shipley's constant battle for self-knowledge. Her struggles with the mirror demonstrate how she perceives her physicality to bind and mediate the subjectivity from which she speaks and that she offers to readers to share. Hagar recognizes that, with the exception of her eyes, her body is growing old: "I am past ninety, and this figure seems somehow arbitrary and impossible, for when I look in my mirror and beyond the changing shell that houses me, I see the eyes of Hagar Currie, the same dark eyes as when I first began to remember and to notice myself" (Laurence 1964, 38). To her there is a self beyond the physical manifestation she views in the mirror; she does not reconcile herself with her body but rather imagines it to be a temporary and mutable shelter. She later clings to a youthful body image that forgets the "changing shell" she has earlier acknowledged: "Yet now," she says long after she has left Manawaka, "I feel that if I were to walk carefully up to my room, approach the mirror softly, take it by surprise, I would see there again that Hagar with the shining hair, the dark-maned colt off to the training ring" (42). Just as Hagar's eyes refuse to change, so too does her "I" upon which readers wholly rely—she will not internalize her unreliable appearance. Doing so would be to accept the social pity she has so long disdained and to incorporate a representational framework that limits her body to decrepitude. To reconcile with the biological changes time has wrought would be to succumb to the cultural meaning that old age incurs. Through devastating figures of speech, quite opposite to the young horse to which she compares her young self, she distances herself from the physical aspects of aging that are so frequently read as the entire experience.

Hagar presents herself as having a mind at odds with her body, reflecting the metaphoric separation embedded in her linguistic expression. Faced with the possibility of exile to a nursing home, she describes herself as divided: "I am overcome with fear, the feeling one has when the ether mask goes on, when the mind cries out to the limbs, 'flail against the thing,' but the limbs are already touched with lethargy, bound and lost" (95). Hagar has trouble unifying even her own subjectivity: "Yet I glance down at myself all the same . . . and see with surprise and unfamiliarity the great swathed hips. My waist was twenty inches when I wed" (56). Hagar presents herself as unable to reconcile her mental strength with her perceived physical diminishment to the extent that her understanding of her body does not match its physical manifestation. She still expects to see a dark-haired, ambitious young woman in the mirror because she has not yet associated the body presented her by the mirror with herself. Accordingly, she relies on a figure of speech that infinitely defers that recognition so that she can always both be and not be the vehicles she chooses for self-description. The clash between images therefore is no longer a clash between young Hagar and old Hagar but instead a disjunction between filly and "mare" (31); the metaphors offer readers a distance from aging human flesh and a new visual emphasis. Just as Hagar gradually adjusts to myriad physical changes, readers must renegotiate the complex metaphorical terrain as it shifts from present to past (as viewed through the present).

Despite the supposedly deep-seated belief that she is still the young, striking Hagar, whose "good bones don't change" (283), Laurence's character continually describes herself by means of bestial cow, crustacean, and fish metaphors that shield her from accepting her "changing shell" while they reinforce how she is mired within it. Hagar's bestial self-representation bathetically foregrounds her body at a time when it is most unreliable. Trying to translate her body into a linguistic reality, which could somehow signal a mental acceptance accompanied by a resistance to change, instead results in a constant distancing—to accept her horrifying flesh as her own would be to acknowledge her own mortality. Remaining in a metaphoric realm, however, implies an acceptance of the self's invisibility and absence (in that other terms continually take its place). Further, the indignity associated with the betrayal of Hagar's body signals and even symbolizes a broader loss of control, not just linguistically but also in terms of her mobility, which denotes freedom. Ultimately she cannot escape physically because she wants to leave behind the decay and unreliability of her body and also the entire social construction (which she continues to play into) that considers aged flesh useless. Ironically, the very unreliability of her body sabotages her escape attempt. Readers cannot follow Hagar on the expected road trip because they learn from the constant bathos and contradictory self-descriptions that limits will be imposed. As does Hagar, readers must restrict triumphs to mental reconstructions and seemingly miniscule physical victories, such as remembering not to drink that late-night cup of potentially treacherous tea.

Hagar's yearning for respectability, ingrained at an early age, permeates her relationships and undermines her marriage. Throughout the novel, her continued desire to meet with approval manifests itself in her concern with apparel. When she is angry with the doctor, she wishes she had not accorded him the respect obvious in having donned her lilac silk: "Now I wish I'd worn my oldest cotton housedress, the one that's ripped under the arms, and not bothered to comb my hair at all" (91). Hagar's attitude toward her clothing, however, reveals a desire not just to meet with general approval but also to be considered attractive. On seeing her husband Bram again after their separation, she describes her choice of clothing as redeeming her overweight body: "I was too padded on the hips and bust, but the dress was becoming, a green cotton with pearl buttons down the front, a dress I'd bought in the autumn sales last fall" (170). Further, Hagar actually attempts to blame the lack of appropriate attire for her girth: "I will maintain until my dying day that it was the lack of a foundation garment" (56). At the same time as she tacitly recognizes her swollen frame as her own, she works to externalize the cause of her physical mutation. She desperately tries to control her changing body, to keep it in check with clothing, at the same time as she blames external forces for its mutation so as not to be responsible for a horrific transformation.

One of the few times Hagar speaks of her body unmediated by overt figurative language, her continued desire for sex, which she paradoxically craved and resented, manifests itself as a secret that she has finally, in the present narrative, shared. Certainly she never told Bram of her own physical pleasure: "It was not so very long after we wed, when first I felt my blood and vitals rise to meet his. He never knew. I never let him know. I never spoke aloud, and I made certain that the trembling was all inner" (81). That Bram would never even suspect Hagar had "sucked [her] secret pleasure from his skin," even when she was a relatively young woman, perhaps makes even more shocking her consequent admission of continued desire for him (100). Readers must confront the sexuality of a body not often thought of as sexual, and they must adjust to heated sexual desire in a character they have grown to know as extraordinarily circumspect. Hagar's protracted lust emerges from under the fabric of metaphor that attempts to remove her from her age. The glimmer of physical desire defies the very cultural stereotypes of aging, associated with the body, that she refuses to take on herself.

Hagar's late-life desire, however, presents itself as a source of shame only because her own ageism renders Bram's body withered and pathetic in her eyes: "His shoulders were stooped, and his wide spade-beard had become only a tufted fringe along his face. When he looked at me, his eyes were mild and milky, absent of expression. And I, more than anything, was doubly shamed recalling how I'd thought of him at night these past years" (171–72). Hagar here (and elsewhere) buys into the models of socially constructed images of bodies and no longer finds Bram sexually desirable because she perceives him as grotesque in his aged manifestation (which has not been the object of her fantasies about him). Just as she fights, through metaphor, recognizing her own aging body, Bram stays young in her mind. When Hagar describes Bram's body to readers in such pejorative terms, she hints at her own decrepitude, but again without directly confronting herself or her audience.

Scrutiny, for Hagar, is closely linked to societal sanction. Ultimately Hagar cannot escape visual scrutiny, nor can she cloak it in metaphor or clothing because she knows that she relies on it to an extent for her survival. Rather than symbolizing her need to be free from her son Marvin and daughter-in-law Doris's aid (on which she physically depends), her desire for physical escape actually symbolizes her contradictory need for both mental freedom and control: "My head is lowered, as I flee their scrutiny, but I cannot move, and now I see that in this entire house, mine, there is no concealment. How is it that all these years I fancied violation meant an attack upon the flesh?" (74) Violation, which for so many years was tangled up in her complicated physical relations with her husband, Bram, finally more clearly operates mainly on a psychological level. Now that her body is not one that society considers sexual, Hagar's fears shift to protective privacy—she wants to hide her transformation even if she has to flee everyone she knows to do so.

As Alice Bell has noted, incontinence signals all of the betrayals of Hagar's body (1996, 52-53). Besides Hagar's acknowledgement of orgasm, constipation and incontinence are the closest to literal descriptions of her body the reader receives from her narration, but in fact each bodily function acts as a metaphor for equally unsuccessful and distressing emotional strategies. When Doris informs Hagar that she has been wetting the bed, Hagar is mortified not just by the utter loss of control, but also by the fear that she did not realize the extent to which she had lost physical control. The final scenes, set in a hospital, depend upon urinary function and the ability to gain a bedpan independently. Hagar's ultimate triumph results from her escaping a straitjacket in order to offer bladder relief to a younger generation. Because readers have learned Hagar's metaphoric lexicon, they can understand how her physical incontinence signifies a similar loss of narrative control, so that Hagar is in fact almost predictable in her unreliability as a narrator.

The constant threat of falling best exemplifies how Hagar's body thwarts her design and ultimately confines her. Although Hagar's desire for physical, mental, bodily, and social escape runs throughout narratives of both the past and the present, almost every time she tries to stand up (in the present), she risks falling. Trying to flee the institution, Silverthreads, Hagar worries about her ability: "Down the steps I go, hoping my legs won't let me down. I grip the railing with both hands, feeling my way ahead, testing each step with a cautious foot like someone wading into a cold sea" (Laurence 1964, 105). Early in the present-tense narrative, Doris and/or Marvin come to her aid each time she tries to stand on her cramped feet, but when she finally achieves, however briefly, the physical distance she craves, her fear of falling nonetheless confines her to her bed: "My feet, still shod, are clenched with cramp. I should rise and stand, work the muscles straight. I daren't, though. What if I fall? Who'd tote me up?" (161). Her final stance, rising to give a copatient a bedpan so that the young woman might be spared the indignity that Hagar experiences as a matter of aged course, doubly (if only momentarily) conquers the bodily limits, metaphorical and actual, to which she gradually succumbs. Not only does she stand without falling, but her aged bodily presence also offers control to a younger manifestation. Hagar feels helpless, yet offers help, underscoring that although her increasingly diminished mobility highlights her need for escape, her mental strength engages with her failing physicality to achieve a new sense of self. Readers are still left to question the degree to which the falls are metaphoric indications of failed narrative strategies.

The only control Hagar can even try to maintain is linguistic, so that she chooses a bodily figure of speech to describe the tenuous hold she maintains on expression: "But when I try to think what it is I'd impart, it's gone, it's only been wind that swelled me for an instant with my accumulated wisdom and burst like a belch" (234). At the very moments when her lack of mobility makes communication imperative, the increasing unreliability of her mind (accompanied and expressed by the unreliability of her body) hampers verbal exchanges. All she can do is figuratively evoke the changes that she cannot control. Similarly, Hagar's own heart becomes a figure for her own reckless need for escape, which, even if it could possibly succeed, could end only in self-destruction because she, like her heart, tries to flee what sustains her. Hagar's constant struggle for control plays out within her ribcage as she fights to contain what, like her, is determined to escape: "My heart is pulsing too fast, beating like a berserk bird. I try to calm it. I must, I must, or it will damage itself against the cage of bones. But still it lurches and flutters, in a frenzy to get out" (95).

Ultimately, Hagar can escape only linguistically, and even her linguistic escape is only the choice to speak figuratively rather than literally. Her desire and increasing need for escape from the social constructions of her aging thematically unify the novel in the way that critics who argue biblical references and feminism do. Hagar's specific investment in figurative language results from her experience of aging flesh, and so the various events and vignettes that make up the novel are unified by a specific mode of representation that directly results from the protagonist and narrator's age. For example, she describes herself as "a slow old sway-back," "gasp[ing] and flouder[ing] like a slimed fish on a dock," "fixed and fluttering, like an earthworm impaled by children on the ferociously unsharp hook of a safety pin," and "glar[ing] like an old malevolent crow" (31, 31, 54, 91). In Hagar's negative descriptive figures, the vehicles are bestial and derogatory, and the tenor continually shifts and evades readers. Laurence tackles crucial issues of late life by adopting a densely figurative register that illuminates the troubling assumptions that too frequently gird depictions of old women.

The Stone Angel coalesces to provide a coherent vision of how physical limitations and mental struggles circumscribe an aging, ill woman's world. Hagar's remarkable, and momentarily successful, escape attempt, when she runs away to the cannery, literally and metaphorically enacts a journey she has always desired and never been free enough to attempt. Hagar Shipley offers the only conduit to knowledge for readers of *The Stone Angel.* Concentrating on the narration of that novel shifts how the present-tense story, through which the past is refracted, frames not only the fiction but also its criticism. The careful layering of narrative and deliberate metaphoric evasions expands readers' cultural understanding of late life. The distinct narrative voice compels readers to recognize Hagar Shipley as old, and beyond that as a particular, historically situated, culturally determined individual woman in late life. Readers are not likely to continue their engagement with *The Stone Angel* by presuming all old women to be similar to Hagar, but rather the process of reading should present them with the vast, little studied, and rarely understood interior negotiations associated with each and every aging body.

Conclusion

De Beauvoir and Laurence present narrators who devastatingly criticize their physical form and present their own bodies as grotesque in the way that readers will likely expect. Limited narration puts the narrator fascinated by aging in direct conversation with readers who must follow and work around the cues provided. Age and especially current social understandings of age provide the perfect excuse for an unreliable narrator—forgetfulness and misreadings of one's own physical change guide a questionable framing of age. This unreliability could play a liberatory role, as it does in the novels Gullette celebrates, but for de Beauvoir and Laurence, the unreliability at best draws attention to the forces that create harmful perceptions of aging. The intensely ambivalent depictions of age result from an emphasis on physical change and on how women often construct self-worth through an understanding of their own beauty and sexual desirability.

During her brief escape to the cannery, Hagar Shipley happens upon dead June bugs that she admires for their beauty: "Their backs are green and luminous, with a sharp metallic line down the center, and their bellies shimmer with pure copper. If I've unearthed jewels, the least I can do is wear them" (216). She adorns her hair with her newfound treasure and imagines herself to be an Egyptian princess. Long after she has forgotten her fantasy, Murray Lees invades her hideout, and Hagar, as is her habit, struggles to look appropriate: "I put up a hand to straighten my hair. My fingers meet something brittle. I pinch it—it squashes and snaps under my nail and smells putrid. Then I recall the June bugs and could die with mortification" (220). Left to her own devices, Hagar can transform the seemingly useless bug shells into a fantastic ornament, but when she has to see herself through someone else's eyes, the bug shells become disgusting. A chasm reopens between the indefatigable, recalcitrant Hagar and the worn-out, defeated Hagar. In one scene she has the strength to reimagine her old age; in the next she succumbs to it.

Simone de Beauvoir and Margaret Laurence explore battles with self-perception at the same time as they participate in a familiar denigration of old age. Their characters' most telling moments occur in front of the mirror that they perceive to confront them with a reality they yearn to deny. The resulting physical descriptions invest in devastating metaphors of decay that buy into pervading cultural stereotypes and, at best, promote a sympathy for readers with the aging characters. At worst, they incite a fear of one's own impending age. The focus on physical change and its supposedly inevitable interpretation is highly suspect and changeable. More recent narratives of aging shift the focus from the physical and parody the investment in physical change that usually dominates narratives of age.

It is only when Anne Dubreuilh decides to honor her social responsibility as grandmother and psychologist that she really turns away from the mirror that symbolizes her terror of aging. De Beauvoir and Laurence hone in, perhaps unwittingly, on a significant problem for women as they age. When women value themselves for their beauty (currently defined as youth), when they focus on their physical appearance, then age will be especially devastating (until beauty can be redefined). Worry about the social judgment of appearances entails buying into beliefs about socially appropriate appearances. When Hagar shifts her concern to where she will live out her final days, she performs a valiant service to a younger patient and defies the social misconceptions that have previously circumscribed her actions. It is for this reason that as I turn to the more constructive depictions of old age that have followed Laurence's groundbreaking character, I also focus on the social possibilities for old women. A focus on how to live in the world rather than on how the world will perceive one's age promises a movement away from the mirror-gazing trope that pervades most negative stories of age.

Chapter Two

Generation Gaps and the Potential of Grandmotherhood

Considerations of motherhood as an institution and an experience pervade scholarly feminism, and they provide a crucial takeoff point for a discussion of grandmotherhood, the key familial relationship within the texts I study. The cultural standards and pressures that restrict motherhood are not yet as well articulated in connection with grandmotherhood, so it may be possible that grandmaternity presents an alternate conceptualization for female-female love. In the introduction to *Mother of My Mother: The Intricate Bond between Generations,* written for a general audience, Hope Edelman offers a comprehensive summary of current writing about grandmotherhood: "My findings were closely aligned with what other researchers had revealed: . . . that the granddaughter-grandmother relationship can absorb more ambivalence than the mother-daughter relationship; and that many women feel they have more in common with their maternal grandmothers than they do with their mothers" (1999, 9). In this chapter I turn to two Canadian novels that encapsulate the ambivalences that can thrive within a grandmother-granddaughter relationship whereas they may trouble a mother-daughter bond.

Old age is not a necessary prerequisite for grandmaternity, nor is grandmaternity a necessary prerequisite for becoming an old woman. However, for certain old women, the possibilities offered through grandmotherhood could defy past understandings of their appropriate female role as well as present understandings of their age identity. Although perhaps exemplary, a First Nations' influence is not really an appropriate starting place for this study because to claim that these cultural conceptions affect other North American social groups to any large extent would be inaccurate. To pretend otherwise, I fear, would be to appropriate the positive aspects of a particular complex and misunderstood storytelling legacy and even belief system (because the elderly are deified by some First Nations' groups and by few other Canadian cultural subgroups). In the novels discussed here, and in much of the Canadian nonnative context, culture, love, knowledge, and potential freedom are transmitted between female relatives within the existing and confining framework of the nuclear family. Beginning with *The Stone Angel*, moving through contemporary criticism on motherhood and opening into two recent novels that rethink family boundaries, I explore how convoluted interfemale family relationships can be, especially when a daughter becomes a mother and has to play both social roles, pushing her own mother into the new role of grandmother. Most important, that complexity, in contrast with the ambivalence of de Beauvoir's and Laurence's portraits of old age, is constructive of new approaches to age identity, so the grandmother-granddaughter relationship is a site of great potential.

Extraordinarily negative depictions of old women as relentless, matriarchal family heads (ultimately undermined) or doting, witless grandmothers and great aunts, treated nicely out of a politeness born of condescension rather than respect, permeate fiction and film. Widespread denigration of old women and a general lack of academic studies of their social, and especially familial, influence indicate that such objectionable characterizations not only reflect general negative opinions and fear but may also dictate them. Narrative's normativity influences the way in which old women can be portrayed because to alter their depiction might bestow upon them a social power that threatens established cultural dynamics. Old women are so consistently undervalued that to conceive of a crucial familial role for them requires a systematic change in what is even imaginable. Reimagining grandmotherhood might contribute to discourses of aging that resist or at least enrich the pervasive cultural narratives of decline.

Hagar Shipley and the Role of Grandmother

Toward the end of *The Stone Angel*, after she is hospitalized, the distance between the Egyptian princess Hagar with emerald jewels in her hair and the ailing old woman Hagar with squashed June bugs on her head narrows. Once she accepts her confinement, the same imagination that allows her to forget momentarily (in the cannery) how her age is perceived allows her to transfer her desires for escape onto a distanced generation. When she hands her copatient Sandra Wong a bedpan, she is simultaneously strong and old. The union of her past defiance and her present need arises at least partly from her ability to imagine that her own granddaughter's experiences will exceed her own.

Hagar had not anticipated that the offspring of her own disappointment would play the role in her life that she does: "I couldn't have guessed then that my granddaughter Tina would become so dear to me" (1964, 183). The glimpses Hagar offers readers of her relationship with Tina further reflect, even in their brevity, the thwarted desire for escape she faces throughout the novel. The person in her life who could enact the escape for which she longs always remains slightly out of reach—for readers and Hagar alike. As a result, readers (and possibly Hagar) do not have enough information to determine whether Tina's imminent wedding will differ significantly from Hagar's. Readers and Hagar learn from Steven (Hagar's grandson) that Tina will remain out east to marry. Readers cannot determine, however, whether that escape resembles Hagar's own misguided self-imposed exile to the Shipley farm or whether Tina's future has new potential. That the youngest female generation remains just barely outside the purview of the novel suggests some form of escape. Readers can merely imagine what kind of continuation the absent character of Tina might provide and further speculate what kind of unique benefits both women could reap from a grandmother-granddaughter connection.

Hagar, in this one case, has managed to avoid her usual controlling role in the life of a person who could actualize her dreams. In *The Second Sex,* de Beauvoir offers a best-case scenario for grandmotherhood: "Recognizing neither rights nor responsibilities, she loves them in pure generosity; she does not indulge in narcissistic dreams through them, she demands nothing of them, she does not sacrifice to them a future she is never to see" (1971, 556). De Beauvoir suggests that once elderly women relinquish their own battles with circumstances, they can perhaps accept that the liberty they have not been able to achieve may to some extent be embodied by a subsequent generation (if that generation exists within their families). Facing perhaps different cultural restraints from those that bind motherhood, they may be in a position to offer unselfish devotion to their grandchildren. Erik H. Erikson, Joan M. Erikson, and Helen Q. Kivnick put the possibility differently, saying in *Vital Involvement in Old Age,* "Grandparenting, since it is the culmination of the parenting role, seems to offer elders one of the most positive and vital involvements of old age" (1986, 306). Though by no means automatic, the possibility exists for grandmotherhood to confer a new mode of engaging. Laurence conveys this in her characterization of Hagar, who is considerably more emotionally generous to her grandchildren than to her children.

At a loss for words, Hagar surprises her son and daughter-in-law with the gesture of passing on her own mother's ring to Tina: "I haven't a word to send her, my granddaughter. Instead, I tug at my right hand, pull and shake, and finally wrench off the ring" (Laurence 1964, 279). At last, in relation to her granddaughter, Hagar appears emotionally generous. The passing on of her mother's ring is frequently read as Hagar's acceptance of a matriarchal lineage. Constance Rooke appropriately interprets it as linking four generations of women (1982, 41). Most important, the ring marks a cross-generational connection more than any connection between immediate generations. Helen Buss argues that Hagar's "gentle feelings toward Tina signal a new stage in her life, one that is to bring her closer to the mother and the values represented by that figure" (1985, 12). Perhaps the giving of the ring indicates reconciliation with Hagar's own mother and not, as Cynthia Taylor and Buss argue, reconciliation with the archetypal mother image. However, Hagar best matches the largely unrecognized archetypal grandmother capable of love without possession and without expectation of return, evoked by Simone de Beauvoir in *The Second Sex*. When Taylor explains that "Hagar comes to realize that she has been wandering in the wilderness, and her gift of the ring is her attempt to pass on the love, confirmation, and example which she lacked," she pinpoints a crucial aspect of the role of grandmother that Hagar accepts (1996, 169). If only momentarily, Hagar indulges in what de Beauvoir calls "pure generosity." When she receives her grandson in the hospital room, her reaction indicates the kind of nonpossessive love that also most likely marks the passing on of the ring.

At the very least, Hagar's grandson thinks of her as generous. He reminds her that she used to give him money for candy, prompting her to recognize yet another way others perceive her: "That's what I am to him—a grandmother who gave him money for candy. What does he know of me? Not a blessed thing" (Laurence 1964, 296). She has played a beneficent grandmother role without investing it with her own particular agency, and she perceives this as a lack. She tries to bridge the gap by asking an uncharacteristic question about Steven's current happiness but receives an unsatisfactory response. She can only content herself with his professional success by means of which she can partially acquit her son and daughter-in-law for their other perceived failings. At the very least, a satisfaction with her grandson mediates her dissatisfaction with her son. She has achieved as a grandmother what she never could as a mother.[1]

Motherhood and Grandmotherhood

De Beauvoir's discussion of grandmotherhood in *Second Sex* is not entirely positive. She fully recognizes that as women age they may well become more resentful of their position as women in the world and that this resentment could affect their relationships with female family members: "The older the child gets, the more does resentment gnaw at the mother's heart; each year brings her nearer her decline, but from year to year the young body develops and flourishes; it seems to the mother that she is robbed of this future which opens before her daughter" (1971, 491). In some cases, Simone de Beauvoir claims, a mother fights the possibility that her daughter could take on the role of mother, further supplanting her position within the family. In contradiction to her postulation of serene benevolence, she also argues that "the feelings of the grandmother toward her grandchildren are extensions of those she feels toward her daughter, and she frequently transfers her hostility to them" (555). It is only if a grandmother can "[retain] a warm affection for her grandchildren while renouncing complete possession, [that] she can play the privileged role of guardian angel in their lives" (556).

As indicated by de Beauvoir's model of the extension of maternal hostility, her discussion of motherhood is impressively negative. She begins the chapter titled "The Mother" with a lengthy discussion of abortion. The ensuing analysis of the situation of pregnancy emphasizes what Adrienne Rich later expands: the physicality of motherhood. De Beauvoir describes the physicality of pregnancy as perceived from without: "Ensnared by nature, the pregnant woman is plant and animal, a stockpile of colloids, an incubator, an egg; she scares children proud of their young, straight bodies and makes young people titter contemptuously because she is a human being, a conscious and free individual, who has become life's passive instrument" (467). As is the case with de Beauvoir's explanation of the physicality of old age, she evaluates the way in which that external interpretation of the pregnant body affects the pregnant woman's self-perception: "But pregnancy is above all a drama that is acted out within the woman herself. She feels it at once an enrichment and an injury; the fetus is a part of her body, and it is a parasite that feeds on it; she possesses it, and she is possessed by it; it represents the future and, carrying it, she feels herself vast as the world; but this very opulence annihilates her, she feels that she herself is no longer anything" (466). She explores how the resulting situation of motherhood becomes especially dramatic when a woman is mother to a daughter. Her analysis leads directly to the previously cited discussion of grandmotherhood, which, though still mired in the physicality of motherhood (the aging mother compares her body to the younger daughter), does not have physical markers in and of itself. Later theorists of motherhood mitigate de Beauvoir's negativity to some degree, but they do not follow her lead in investigating the implications of the related role of grandmotherhood.

Adrienne Rich's *Of Woman Born* discusses motherhood as institution distinct from what she calls "the potential relationship" many women could have with their reproductive capacity and their children (1986, 13). Patriarchy restricts the latter (potential) within the former (institution) so that reproduction and any possible associated power remains firmly within male control. For Rich, the act of giving birth symbolizes the social situation of the institution of motherhood. Women as mothers are expected to efface themselves to the extent that even if they do not die giving birth, their physical death in labor can be replaced by a figurative one: "Yet, even in a place and time where maternal mortality is low, a woman's fantasies of her own death in childbirth have the accuracy of metaphor. Typically, under patriarchy, the mother's life is exchanged for the child; her autonomy as a separate being seems fated to conflict with the infant she will bear" (166). Motherhood, in this view, means possible elimination of womanhood; in giving birth, a mother risks cultural erasure as a woman and yet visibly takes on the role that patriarchal society typically requires of women. Such direct erasure is neither expected nor likely in the case of grandmother-grandchild relationships. Oddly, perhaps because old people, and especially women, are not thought to possess much social value, they are not expected to relinquish identity in order to love grandchildren. A grandmother's life is rarely exchanged for the child's. Accordingly, grandmothers may be able to maintain whatever emotional autonomy they have been able to gain and still play a formative role in the lives of children by passing on a cultural heritage in the form of stories, lessons, and love. A rich discourse on grandmotherhood does not currently exist, except in a nascent form, such as that in the narrative fiction that I study. One aspect of the institutionalization of grandmotherhood that merits careful articulation is the way in which a grandmother's distinct link to a grandchild resounds symbolically in a larger cultural world. Hand in hand with that unique connection comes the displacement of cultural identity onto an aging body. Parents attribute the need for cultural rituals ("don't lick your knife; your grandmother would turn over in her grave") to another generation rather than take responsibility themselves.

Along with the effacement required of mothers, Rich argues that an antagonism between immediate generations dictated by patriarchal control of motherhood discourages women from desiring maternity (251). Matrophobia, the fear of *becoming* one's own mother, further intensifies the conflict that can develop between mother and daughter. Particularly in the twentieth century, because of rapid developments within feminist thought and activism, daughters often become frustrated with the limitations they see their mothers accepting and become increasingly unable "to see beyond her to the forces acting upon her" (235). Further, even though patriarchal constraints supposedly dictate motherhood structurally, if the practice fails, the mother herself takes the blame and the patriarchal limitations placed upon her role evade it. Rich explains that mothers are expected to represent individual examples of failure to adhere to impossible ideology: "Under the institution of motherhood, the mother is the first to blame if theory proves unworkable in practice, or if anything whatsoever goes wrong" (222). Judgment of mothering falls on the mother regardless of who takes care of the children and regardless of whence mothers derive their mothering practices. Grandmothers too may be socially embarrassed by the behavior of their grandchildren, but the reaction is more likely to be pity that the old woman must tolerate the bad parenting of her daughter or daughter-in-law. (In the first instance she would of course be responsible for not having trained her own daughter as a capable mother.)

Rich recognizes the social separation of motherhood from the physical when she states, "But before we were mothers, we have been, first of all, women, with actual bodies and actual minds" (192). Nonetheless, however ideological motherhood as an institution may become, women continually have to battle perceptions of their physical beings because of a longstanding association of women with the body. As Rich's own study reinforces, becoming a mother reinscribes the body because it is the physical process of giving birth that undeniably cannot be completely usurped by male power. She asserts, "I know no woman—virgin, mother, lesbian, married, celibate—whether she earns her keep as a housewife, a cocktail waitress, or a scanner of brain waves—for whom her body is not a fundamental problem: its clouded meaning, its fertility, its desire, its so-called frigidity, its bloody speech, its silences, its changes and mutilations, its rapes and ripenings" (285). Though all female bodies struggle with physicality, motherhood creates its own specific problems with bodies because of its very signification of fertility, desire, changes, and what is frequently considered as ripening, all of which challenge the sleek, contained form classically deemed beautiful. The fact of having given birth, or being pregnant, has visible physicality that forces others to understand (and frequently repress acknowledging) women who become mothers as sexual and mutable. Though women who become grandmothers likely have faced the complications of what Rich calls ripening, grandmotherhood does not in itself signify fertility the way that motherhood does. And, although old women so frequently confront countless discouraging cultural readings of physical change, no physical changes are directly related to the *role* of grandmother. Becoming a grandmother does not signify sexuality as becoming a mother can, partly because of a social reluctance to conceive of old people as sexual. Still, though old women may battle numerous physical problems, actual and those projected upon them, none appear as the result of their new familial role as grandmother. Despite the frequently brutal effects (social and physical) of physical change on old women, grandmotherhood typically does not intensify struggles with body image as motherhood does.

When Rich discusses potential roles for older women, she hints that grandmotherhood could provide an escape route from the confining and problematic pressures enforced by maternity. She refers to her own family to explain: "My mother lives today as an independent woman, which she was always meant to be. She is a much-loved, much-admired grandmother, an explorer in new realms; she lives in the present and future, not the past" (224). The role of grandmother has much of the potential that has been sapped from that of mother. This is not to deny the considerable scholarly work that reimagines motherhood so that it no longer denotes a compliance with a patriarchal authority structure, but rather to explore an as yet underconsidered alternate model for female relations. Rich, in describing her mother, implies that becoming and being a grandmother offers the potential for being loved and admired in a manner that is not limited by the inability of children and grandchildren to see beyond the forces that work upon mothers. It is much easier, by virtue of physical and temporal distance, to recognize forces acting on grandmothers as external and to appreciate difference and similarity across the boundaries of family divisiveness. Further, in the absence of a general social tendency to require grandparenthood from women, there is greater freedom in shaping the role so that it can encompass a variety of emotional and cultural possibilities, perhaps even outside the patriarchal constraints that dominate Rich's configuration of motherhood (especially because it may be articulated in an era dominated to some degree by feminist discourse—it is feminists who are most likely to explore fully the potentials of grandmotherhood).

The emotional and cultural possibilities expected of maternity are enormous and usually untenable, whether formulated in keeping with or in opposition to patriarchal constraints. Sara Ruddick's exploration of maternal thinking as a possible model for nonviolence places an oddly large burden on mothers despite its reflexivity about the problems associated with increasing mothers' responsibilities in such a way. *Maternal Thinking: Toward a Politics of Peace* (1995) emphasizes living as a mother more than *Of Woman Born* (1986), which concentrates on pregnancy and labor. Still, Ruddick's extension of the work of motherhood into a realm of peace politics fixes such a high value on a maternal perspective that she leaves little room for women (or men who choose to mother) to have other occupations or preoccupations. Whereas Rich presents poetry as offering her a space (as she figures it) separate from motherhood—"For me, poetry was where I lived as no-one's mother, where I existed as myself" (1986, 31)—Ruddick's valuation of the maternal leaves no such role-free space. The danger of being continually expected to mother, regardless of actual relationship, increases rather than decreases if a world view (such as pacifism) entirely depends on the values of motherhood, whether or not they are drastically rewritten.

Ruddick reiterates, in the introduction to her second edition, the importance of maternal *work* that she claims anyone can perform regardless of biological function. As with Rich's distinction between the institution of motherhood and the potential inherent in women's relationships, Ruddick distinguishes an oppressive "mother*hood*" from maternity, which does not have to entail the kinds of sacrifices generally associated with the "consuming identity" usually required of mothers (1995, 29). For Ruddick, a mother must be centrally preoccupied by working for "*preservation, growth,* and *social acceptability*" on the part of a child (17). In a sense she speaks of motherhood as an occupation similar to any other wherein there is room for failure, evaluation, and anger. However, by making mothering an ideological occupation and never quite relinquishing idealism, Ruddick generalizes mothering to the extent that it operates as a symbol or goal rather than the practice she tries to make it.

The intergenerational conflict between mothers and daughters that Rich prefigures haunts Ruddick's consideration, particularly because Ruddick fully articulates the extent to which mothers are held responsible for the work they do, as determined by children's behavior and well-being. As Ruddick puts it, "many mothers find that the central challenge of mothering lies in training a child to be the kind of person whom others accept and whom the mothers themselves can actively appreciate" (104). Mothers are judged for their success in preserving, nurturing, and molding their children. Sometimes they take the role of judge onto themselves: "[T]he more personally invested a mother is in her children's acceptable behaviour, and therefore the more rewards she expects from her maternal work, the more angry and ashamed she will be when her influence does not have the desirable effects" (106). According to Ruddick, mothers work with an eye to extravagant blame or praise from grandparents, fathers, and even passersby (111). Further, as with Rich's conceptualization, even when this external praise may be present, there is potential conflict from within the parent-child relationship. Ruddick explains that "daughters are not likely to give up a hard-won, hard-held critical stance" (40). To extend Ruddick's thinking, the tendency of daughters to hold their mothers in ambivalent contempt affects a grandmother in a family setting because she is at once mother and grandmother, but she has another generation to which to direct her attention, and that generation does not have to battle her in the same way to maintain identity. A conflict across generations is not as necessary to child development as a conflict between immediate generations. In other words, though mothers and daughters often fight, grandmothers and granddaughters can become allies in larger battles.

According to Ruddick, mothers are defined as such by the work that they do and leave themselves open to judgment according to how well they are perceived to have achieved the goals of "preservative love, nurturance, and training" (17). Ruddick offers a cursory discussion of *abuelas* ("grandmothers") in a specific historical context but not as a philosophical model. Besides that brief analysis, the only role that grandmothers play explicitly in her study is that of potential critic. They frequently fall into the list of outsiders who will inevitably evaluate the work of the mother. Failing that, they may have actually taken on the maternal work of raising a child, in which case they would be included in Ruddick's use of the term *mother.* I suggest that grandmothers do not have to play the role of mother entirely or centrally in order to have a potentially profound and transformative connection with a particular child or children. Moreover, they can pursue such a relationship without being perceived as morally responsible for the child's demeanor. Because it is not necessary to rewrite the role of grandmother in terms of work to give it value, the criteria of evaluation can be less severe.

Marianne Hirsch's *Mother/Daughter Plot* talks about the problem of female intergenerational conflict by drawing on literature (1989). She works within a psychoanalytic paradigm to tackle the problem of maternal subjectivity (and its lack in literature), particularly in literary convention. In exploring the unspeakability of maternal plots, she suggests the possibility of dual narration to enable a maternal subjectivity to emerge from within what she considers a repression in literary tradition. A dialogue between mothers and daughters would allow both parties in a discordant relation to develop agency and potentially grow to share a voice. She explains, "The multiplicity of 'women' is nowhere more obvious than for the figure of the mother, who is always both mother and daughter. Her representation is controlled by her object status, but her discourse, when it is voiced, moves her from object to subject. But, as long as she speaks as mother, she must always remain the object in her child's process of subject-formation; she is never fully a subject" (12). Ruddick proposes that daughters should begin by listening to mothers without adopting the oppressive conditions that sometimes dictate their roles. Hirsch formulates a narrative strategy that would enable female characters to be constructed as subjects in maternal stories. She suggests a similar starting point to Ruddick's: "Feminism might begin by listening to the stories that mothers have to tell, and by creating the space in which mothers might articulate those stories" (167). Having played a daughterly role and been a subject within that role, feminists, according to Hirsch, might benefit from a resituation in relation to mothers. The new positioning could allow a multiplicity of narrative voices in the story she considers motherhood and daughterhood to be.

All of the reasons for conflict between mother and daughter that Rich, Ruddick, and Hirsch outline suggest that a shared voice (a first person meant to include both a mother and a daughter's perspectives) would contradict itself. Because Hirsch's object-subject paradigm implies that each (mother and daughter) has to oppose the other to establish identity, it is difficult to imagine a harmonious shared voice. On the other hand, a grandmother and granddaughter do not have to cancel each other out to have agency, and a narrative voice shared by those female relatives is more likely to present a constructive worldview that encompasses greater possibility for female mobility and achievement.

Hirsch expresses the painful conflict between immediate generations: "The greatest tragedy that can occur between mother and daughter is when they cease being able to speak and to listen to one another. But what if they inhabit the same body, what if they are the same person, speaking with two voices?" (199) I explore this assertion in connection with narrative situations wherein certain characters are simultaneously mothers and daughters. A problem arises in each case because these mother-daughter characters are trapped, within the narrative, between the two generations (granddaughter and grandmother). In the examples I have chosen, the grandmothers and granddaughters create a meaningful dialogue rather than the conflicting communication that occurs between each of those two generations and the middle generation (between the two sets of mother and daughter). Perhaps the potential for resolution through grandmotherhood, without motherhood's contradictory possessiveness and loss of identity, mitigates Hirsch's tragedy to some degree; if a mother cannot speak or listen to her daughter, perhaps that daughter will bear a daughter who remedies the generation gap. The conflict that Hirsch pinpoints through close readings of key Victorian female-authored fiction is partly ameliorated in a similar interpretation of recent Canadian female-authored fiction.

Joan Barfoot's *Duet for Three* (1985) and Hiromi Goto's *Chorus of Mushrooms* (1994) provide significant insights into motherhood. In multiple voices, they depict the complexities of growing up in relation to women in a family. Beyond that contribution to understanding maternity, each novel reconfigures grandmotherhood explicitly. The novels theorize (and idealize) grandmotherhood as a unique, freeing relationship that builds on the potential of motherhood and escapes its many pitfalls. Barfoot and Goto characterize grandmothers as offering cultural and historical knowledge through an unconditional, loving connection with granddaughters.

Duet for Three and *Chorus of Mushrooms* theorize grandmother-mother-daughter relationships by carefully juxtaposing narrative voices that constantly renegotiate communicative strategies because of differences in physical, social, linguistic, and figurative location. Whereas *The Stone Angel* offers readers only one perspective through which to view extreme old age, *Duet for Three* sets up a conflictual dialogue (or lack thereof) between a mother and a daughter, who is also a mother in turn. Barfoot employs alternate, opposing narrative voices, that of elderly Aggie and her middle-aged daughter June. Accordingly, readers must continually resituate themselves in relation to the dilemma of the novel, whether to place Aggie in an institution. The title reinforces the impossible situation since Barfoot's narrative duet is in fact a trio and each speaking voice attempts to harmonize with and modulate the background voice of the granddaughter/daughter-figure Frances. *Chorus of Mushrooms* is aptly named because of a bizarre layered narration (in at least two languages and including a grocery list) that overtly forces readers to consider many perspectives toward old age. Readers cannot operate on typical assumptions of reliability in the novel, which, though often written in a realist style, is openly presented as a granddaughter's fictional reconstruction of the experiences of a grandmother with whom she did not even share a language. Goto continually reminds readers of the narrative's fictionality. The attempt to narrate a grandmother's life through a granddaughter evokes a crucial connection that can be forged even in the absence of shared culture (and key cultural tools such as language and food).

Joan Barfoot's "Badge of Membership"

Though its voice is mostly third person, *Duet for Three* (1985) alternates between the perspectives of Aggie, an obese, eighty-something, nontraditional grandmother-mother, and June, Aggie's thin, sixty-something, conservative daughter who is herself mother to Frances. Readers accrue awareness of the disjunction between their thinking and of the degree to which the characters cannot communicate past that difference. The alternating narration encourages readers to configure the extent to which interpretation and point of view affect family history.

An overheard narration encapsulates the relationships among the three generations, Aggie as grandmother-mother, June as daughter-mother, and Frances as daughter-granddaughter. Aggie is explaining the problems she encountered with her husband (June's father), a grandfather Frances never knew. Barfoot tucks the entire exchange into parentheses to indicate how the granddaughter and grandmother understand each other to the exclusion of June (mother-daughter):

> ("He was," she said another time when Frances asked, "a man who arranged all his books in alphabetical order. By author."
> ("Yeah," Frances nodded, "I see."
> ("What's that supposed to mean?" asked June. "What's wrong with that?") (80)

From her middle position, June is unable to make a crucial connection with either her mother or her daughter, and the lack of understanding stands out in sharp relief against the silent sympathy that Aggie and Frances share. There is no need to explicate the layers of interpretation as she would have to do for June. The arrangement of books signals a specific commitment to precisely the order June craves but Aggie, and Frances in turn, abhors. Throughout the novel, Frances rejects her mother's desire for propriety and containment in favor of Aggie's continued search for freedom and knowledge.

By giving two generations a voice in a struggle over aging, Barfoot further illuminates the battle for control at a time when it is slipping from the oldest character. The alternation of voices diminishes for Aggie the control Hagar Shipley has at least over the version through which readers must deduce other perspectives. Barfoot creates a narrative situation that evokes the frightening loss of control that the descriptions of physical change and unreliability also signify.

Duet for Three begins *in medias res* with Aggie experiencing an utter loss of control; she wakes amidst the results of her incontinence. Aggie vaguely remembers letting go: "Less sensible is a recollection of warmth, release, relief, a brief steamy kind of comfort, a pungent but not unpleasant smell, lulling her back to sleep. It seemed simple at the time, pleasing to have solved a difficulty, without effort, in the dark" (4). The momentary solution, which leads to embarrassment and possible eviction, lends Aggie fleeting pleasure. She similarly embraces obesity, also a symbol of physical control—and its loss—in the novel. However, her attempt to make her body a site of perceived power backfires because her immense frame imposes her eventual lack of mobility and bodily control, thereby threatening to land her in a nursing home. As Aggie's changing form becomes the terrain upon which June and Aggie fight their mother-daughter battles, readers perceive the ways in which bodies signal danger, change, and conflict. What Aggie hoped would be a locus of control and freedom signifies unmanageable late life to June.

Aggie's and June's conflicting perspectives on Aggie's body encapsulate the two characters' incompatibility. Readers perceive June's typical disgust at the enormity of Aggie's aging body while they understand Aggie's pride in immensity. Hagar Shipley's bathetic metaphors collapse here as Aggie feels that her size invites social sanction: "All this," she says of her pregnancy, "seemed like an initiation into a secret society, her badge of membership in her distended body" (92). Aggie begins a deliberate physical transformation during her pregnancy: "She ate and ate; eating, as the women said, for two. She imagined how healthy this child would be, already so well fed" (93). And her continued obesity becomes a quest not just for the enormity that signifies, to her, power but also an attempt to maintain the "badge of membership" she wore in pregnancy and the signified hope for fulfillment: "She got bigger and bigger. She felt, sometimes, as if her strong and rolling body might contain whole towns and cities, countries and continents, or characters: her own and others that she learned about" (158).

Aggie describes her all-encompassing weight gain with pride: "Her slim belly became plump, then rolling. Her thighs began to ripple, her chin sagged and doubled. Her features, and her feet and hands, came to look tiny against the bulk of the rest of her. She became imposing" (107). June describes her mother as a "fat, old, greedy woman" (20) and extends this as a description of her both physically and mentally: "This greedy old woman eats up a life the same way she consumes a pie" (46). Rather than understanding her mother's weight gain as an attempted appropriation of control, she sees it very much as a decline: "Her mother seemed—unleashed, somehow. More sprawling, as if she'd taken off a girdle, and less capable than before of order and moderation" (123). Indeed, the incontinence that creates the urgent time frame of the novel is the flip side of magnitude, in that Aggie's giant physical status leaves her unable to take care of her giant bodily needs. Aggie has so clearly defined herself by her flesh that its metaphorical and literal expansion contains her.

In her turn, June is unable to attach herself to a daughter who does not share her vision of propriety and success. She resents Aggie's influence on Frances, which she perceives as deliberate and pernicious. As a result, she presents some seemingly unmaternal sentiments about Frances's future: "Did Aggie set out to achieve a granddaughter who thinks only of her own convenience, who refuses difficulties and makes frivolous choices? Probably. But some day Frances will crash, and what will her grandmother have to say to her then? Events even out. Or so June hopes" (67–68). Her daughter's constant flaunting of decorum so exasperates her that she experiences what could be called an unmotherly hope for daughterly failure. In contrast, Aggie takes pride in Frances's ability not only to extend limitations and make personal decisions that result in a mobility and self-assurance new to female members of the family, but also to threaten the desire for propriety that June espouses. The power and control Aggie tries to exert upon her own body, which ultimately backfire, exhibit themselves in Frances to June's chagrin and Aggie's satisfaction.

Barfoot's narrative enacts and comments upon Hirsch's tragedy in that two sets of mother and daughter fail to communicate, resulting in an everlasting debt of love that cannot be paid regardless of the countless other sacrifices the women make for each other (136). However, the lack of genuine communication is only one facet of the ultimate breakdown of maternal relationships in the novel. Because she works within the temporal, spatial, and causal mechanisms of narrative, Barfoot manages to illustrate and enhance multiple associations that explain and explore the complicated negotiations associated with growing old in a culture that adequately values neither women nor age. The extremely short time frame of the novel and the tight spatial confines accentuate the excruciatingly delicate and methodical processes of aging and the accompanying decision-making processes. The plot spans a few days wherein June and Aggie struggle over the new insistence—through bed-wetting—of Aggie's body to be central. Spatially, the plot spans Aggie's home and the nursing home June evaluates. The story spills back much further and speculatively forward through Frances, who is the only character outside the physical reaches of the plot. The incontinence that provides the causal relationships in the plot partly explains the tightly contained and controlled space and time of the narrative. Aggie's decision to eat until she fills the house means the novel itself fills the house and centers on whether she can be moved from that location. As a result, when Aggie concedes that she may have to accept some other solution, such as moving to a nursing home, the novel ends. The control she has exercised over her body, mirrored in the plot structure, is over. The careful containment of narrative elements also mirrors the relationships between the two narrators of the novel. The tight narration offers an almost microscopic view that reflects how neither character can withdraw far enough to develop the understanding crucial to an emotional resolution for each.

There is, however, an emotional release in the cross-generational love that forms between Aggie and Frances. Here Aggie can see the possibilities for fulfillment she has sought. She is freed from responsibility for Frances; she is not socially accountable for her, and Frances grows up at a historical moment when there are simply more opportunities for women to act out the self-fulfilling lives Aggie has so desired. In keeping with the carefully controlled plot structure, Frances offers a freedom and release that keeps her out of the plot entirely. Although her arrival is a key turning point for both June and Aggie, once she arrives (from an outside world that could offer both older women the larger perspective they need to relate better), the novel ends.

The love Aggie feels for Frances surpasses even her own expectations, exceeds the narrative frame, and reveals a new emotional register to her:

> The new creature turned out to be Frances; struggling so hard to be free that June, for whom, Aggie sighed, nothing went smoothly, had to be opened with a knife.
>
> And Aggie discovered love, an abrupt and puzzling emotion. (158)

The love that she had hoped to find with the teacher (her husband) and then with June is finally available to her, perhaps precisely because she is finally connected to someone in a role that is not socially scripted to the same degree as marriage and motherhood: "Was this not what Aggie should have felt, looking down at her own daughter at her breast? . . . This love, now, was in full light, a clear, distinct, distinguishable form, piercing, sharp, and occasionally painful" (159). The different kind of love that Aggie feels for Frances is transformative in that it gives Aggie a hope for fulfillment that she had given up on having. From being described as self-serving, she becomes a woman who can accept continuation as the completion of her own happiness.

Although Aggie sees enough of a similarity between herself and her granddaughter to transfer her hopes onto the younger generation, their potential differences allow her to revel in her granddaughters' possibilities. As she puts it, "she wanted not only different circumstances for Frances, freer than her own and with a universe of choices, but also that Frances herself should be different: more refined and alert, braver and lighter" (159). In contrast to her desire to see June more like her, with "gumption" and a thirst for freedom, Aggie is comfortable hoping for a continuation that includes development when projecting her granddaughter's future. Aggie pinpoints the desired difference as partly historical and influenced by external factors ("different circumstances"): "In her day, Aggie could not have seen a way to break the pattern, to say no, and Frances can. That seems a greater journey than a mere journey from, say, the earth to the moon" (16). Even June who, like Aggie, also faces oppressive expectations and an excessive social pressure for women to be amenable recognizes the difference between how she and Aggie are able to approach Frances: "Aggie seemed to have a point about the influence of simply living in different times. Except she said, 'Take advantage,' while June had to warn, 'Take care'" (193). The distinction between how June and Aggie are able to comprehend and act upon the historical factors that govern Frances's opportunities seems to exceed the historical differences. Aggie, as grandmother, can more easily influence Frances to exhaust the limitations of her world because the octogenarian will not face the social consequences of the younger woman's choices.

Hiromi Goto's "Circle of Sound"

Hiromi Goto's *Chorus of Mushrooms* invests in multiple narrative perspectives that present myriad ways to think about old age across generations and cultures (1994). The novel filters a grandmother's story through a granddaughter who does not even share her language. As does Aggie's, Naoe's elderly body becomes the site for a cultural and intergenerational struggle. Painfully, her granddaughter Murasaki, or Muriel, as her parents are only able to call her, grows up not sharing her grandmother's language, and her grandmother has not learned enough English to make conversation possible. Murasaki creates a history to tell her lover and appropriates numerous subject positions in order to do so. She imagines the various perspectives, particularly that of her grandmother, surrounding her childhood and turns them into stories for her lover. As a result, varying perspective continually haunts the narrative, forcing the reader to imagine both from within, without, and beside the different characters involved in the cultural and generational struggle. The explicit storytelling process within the novel forces readers to take into account that Murasaki's voices are designed for the audience of a young Japanese man, and readers merely overhear them (strangely, in translation). The resulting narrative offers readers vivid, evocative metaphors for Naoe's aging flesh, none of which devalue her body through grotesque juxtaposition.

The middle generation of the Tonkatsu family (Murasaki's parents) decides to unlearn Japanese, with the hopes that doing so will diminish the perceived racial gulf between their family and other people in Nanton. Goto's strategically and playfully layered narration clarifies the pain and complications that choice imposes. For example, adopting the voice of the local newspaper, Murasaki presents the stories told by each generation of women in her family. With respect to Japanese language and culture, her mother, Kay (née Keiko), claims, "It is too confusing for a child to juggle two cultures. Two sets of ideals. If you want a child to have a normal and accepted lifestyle, you have to live like everyone else" (189). Murasaki complains,

> I had a grandmother who could only speak Japanese, but I never spoke with her because I never learned the language. I wasn't given the chance to choose.
>
> I feel a lot of bitterness about how I was raised, how I was taught to behave. I had a lot of questions about my heritage, but they were never answered. (189)

Murasaki's grandmother Naoe adds, "*Jitto mimi o sumashite kiite goran, ironna koe ga kikoeru kara. Kokoro no-mimi o mottetara ne*" (190). Because Goto presumably targets a largely non-Japanese(-Canadian) audience with her Canadian publication, her inclusion of Japanese phonetically transcribed into English characters further emphasizes the gulf Murasaki's parents' difficult choice imposes. Most readers, like Kay and young Murasaki, cannot make the same connection with Naoe as with other characters unless they have a mediator, such as adult Murasaki.

Even when she adopts a supposedly neutral and, at the very least, supposedly consistent journalistic voice, Goto, through Murasaki, reinforces how different subject positions battle with cultural heritage. The polyphonic appeal to readers provides an even more satisfying potential resolution in the link between grandmothers and granddaughters. Also, in the complex fictional world set up by Goto, cultural markers, such as language and food, take the place of communication so that the middle generation is not entirely excluded from the newly configured female relationships. Kay's rejection is necessary to Murasaki's ultimate commitment to learning Japanese culture. In Goto's novel, Naoe's criticisms of Kay's parenting choices resolve at the moment they are expressed in the novel because the fact of Murasaki's narration demonstrates that she has bridged the cultural gulf Kay has imposed.

Kay's decision to unlearn Japanese for the sake of her daughter, and in spite of Obāchan (Naoe), translates not only into her own inability but also Murasaki's. Murasaki feels an inherent lack in her loss of Japanese culture, and it is this loss that she seeks to compensate through her reconstruction of her grandmother's story. She has never understood the words her Obāchan speaks, but because she depicts the two as able to communicate anyway, the young girl learns that language is multivalent—rich in its sound beyond meaning: "I never understood the words she said, but I watched and learned. And I begin my understanding now. Obāchan took another route, something more harmonious. Showed me that words take form and live and breathe among us. Language a living beast" (98–99). The cultural gulf Kay willingly imposes on her daughter in the name of assimilation should increase the generation gap between Murasaki and Naoe, but ultimately it actually intensifies their connection. When Murasaki later learns Japanese as an adult, she uses it to tell her lover her grandmother's story, in defiance of her mother's terrified hopes for her.

Kay desperately wants to assimilate into white Canadian society, so much so that she renders herself incapable of openly recognizing the racism that dictates her choice. When school teachers choose Murasaki to play Alice in Wonderland because of her singing voice, Kay happily agrees to dye her daughter's hair blond so that she will look suitable for the part. Although her mother attributes the desired change to how theatre is supposed to create illusion, Murasaki, even as a child, acknowledges the inherent racism: "'Mom!' I hissed. 'Mom, I changed my mind. I don't want to be Alice anymore. I'll be the Mad Hatter, that way, I can just wear a hat. Or the Cheshire Cat! Cats have slanted eyes. That would work out. Mom?'" (177). The final question at the end of Murasaki's slightly vicious capitulation indicates that Kay understands the problems Murasaki faces better than she is willing to let on. Kay's lack of reaction, which prompts Murasaki's childish insistence on attention and response, continues her refusal to acknowledge part of her culture. To acknowledge her own deliberate avoidance of any identification (or even recognition) of Japanese culture (or depictions of Japanese culture) would be to acknowledge that racism defines and circumscribes Kay's parenting. Further, to fully recognize the choice might lead Kay to face her internalization of that racism, as constantly indicated by her stubborn insistence on assimilation, without acknowledgment of how culture determines that process (performing whiteness).

Kay's struggle pits her against Naoe and Murasaki in such a way that the outer generations connect because of the ridiculous lengths to which she takes her enculturation. The pugnacious assimilation injects Hirsch's tragic situation of noncommunication between mother and daughter with wry humor. When Murasaki explains to Kay her reason for breaking up with white boyfriend Hank, her mother misperceives the offense taken: "'Mom, he wanted to have Oriental sex with me.' 'Oh, well, the Bible says we should wait, ummmm . . . ' she trailed away. Obāchan and I, our eyes collided, and we began to laugh" (124). Whereas the mother cannot relinquish her commitment to specific cultural ideals enough to understand her daughter's perspective, granddaughter and grandmother understand without elaboration what mother-daughter entirely fails to comprehend.

Naoe manages to evade exile to the ever-threatening nursing home, Silver Springs in this particular case, by escaping through the storytelling legacy that Murasaki inherits (a legacy that skips a generation due to her daughter Kay's linguistic denial). The threat of the nursing home looms in the embedded narrative of Goto's novel rather than in the frame, as in Laurence's and Barfoot's works. Because Goto imbues *Chorus of Mushrooms* with the possibilities inherent in folktale and magic realism alongside those of realistic narrative, Naoe's old body is not mired in a specific construction of reality or restricted to a narrow cot such as Hagar's. Murasaki offers a fantastic present-tense situation for her grandmother that figures both women as free spirits, not threatened by any form of confinement (physical, social, or cultural).

Murasaki takes advantage of and simultaneously demonstrates narrative freedom when she sarcastically relates her caustic masking of adolescent pain:

> "What happened to your grandma?"
>
> "She went back to Japan. She got sick of all this snow and dust and up and left. I don't blame her."

> "What happened to your grandma?"
> "She went ape-shit and was raving, frothing at the mouth and she ran naked from the house screaming like the pagan she is."
> "What happened to your grandma?"
> "She started to grow fur all over her body and at first we thought it was a symptom of illness or something like she wasn't eating enough so her body was compensating with fur to keep her warm but we found she was actually a *tanuki* who had assumed the form of a woman so she could marry my grandfather because he had set her free from a trap and she wanted to thank him by becoming his wife, but now, she wanted to return to the wilds whence she came." (88–89)

By once again repeating a story with incremental variations, Goto evokes the agony of schoolyard racism and demonstrates how Murasaki deliberately misleads listener(s) in an attempt to evoke a new, full understanding of her grandmother's quest. The method and this example also provide clues as to how both Murasaki and Goto are fully willing to play on, and thereby expose as ridiculous and untenable, the racist assumptions of their audience. Further, the free adaptation of story details to fit circumstances and mock reader expectations enables Murasaki to be free in her description of Naoe's improbable escape. Murasaki promises to "[make] up the truth as [she] goes along" and in doing so releases her grandmother's body from a representational language that would contain and restrict it to one of "non"-reproductive value (12). Because, in her relation of adolescent playground defensiveness, Murasaki has demonstrated her tendency to adapt a story to readers' assumptions, her choice to narrate Naoe's unlikely career as an octogenarian rodeo star also comments on readers' expectations. Readers are set up to accept such late-life freedom and excitement as possible.

Murasaki figures Naoe as lamenting the loss her daughter chooses to inflict on herself and her family. The old woman's voice demonstrates a clear understanding of the cultural divide in her condemnation of Kay's attempted assimilation: "My daughter who has forsaken identity. Forsaken! So biblical, but it suits her, my little convert" (13). She also understands better than Keiko, as she calls Kay, that although denying Murasaki knowledge of Japanese culture removes her from her heritage, learning and speaking Canadian English will not provide access to a cultural heritage because of the complicating factor of how race is perceived: "A child from my heart, a child from my body, but not from my mouth. The language she forms on her tongue is there for the wrong reasons. You cannot move into a foreign land and call that place home because you parrot the words around you" (48). Language can be and is formative and influential within the novel, but Murasaki through Naoe explains that a specific engagement with language is necessary to enact change and that merely mimicking words does not suffice.

Murasaki's reimagination of Naoe's linguistic power enables a self-description that avoids Hagar Shipley's grotesque elision of her old body with bestial decay: "When I was young and beautiful, my lips were an ornament upon my face. Now my face is crumpled with care and seams adorn my cheeks. My mouth bursts wide and the words rush out, a torrent of noise and scatters. An old woman on a wooden chair might not be much to look at, but step inside her circle of sound and fall into a tornado" (24). Naoe, even in self-description, denies the stasis restraining Hagar and Aggie by investing instead in a metaphor of movement and power that begins with her constant barrage of sound. She defines her presence aurally more than visually, so that when she escapes (achieves mobility), it is the silence more than anything else that marks her absence.

Naoe craves the dialogue that Murasaki imagines for her, saying, "I mutter and mutter and no one to listen. I speak my words in Japanese and my daughter will not hear them. The words that come from our ears, our mouths, they collide in the space between us" (4). Kay misinterprets her mother's stubborn refusal to conform to the Canadian plan, reading her choice as contempt: "'You sit there and mutter and taunt me in Japanese just for spite,' Keiko hisses from the crack between the kitchen door and frame, one eye stabbing me through the tiny space" (21). The connection that Naoe maintains for the entire family to a cultural heritage not easily elided does not become evident or crucial until an eerie and unexpected silence marks her absence from the transplanted home (not only have the Tonkatsus been transplanted, but the house they live in has been physically transported and damaged in the process). There are no more Japanese words after Naoe runs away—until Murasaki takes on her role.

Because of her desperation to assimilate into white Canadian society, once her mother leaves home, Kay's only remaining link to Japanese culture disappears. Unable to escape her racialized body and also unable to free her daughter from the same construction, she chooses to abandon the Japanese language almost entirely, in an attempt to sever her own daughter from a derogatory association. Nevertheless, while keeping her mother in her house, Kay manages to maintain some hold on what she has rejected—Naoe represents a channel to a collective past, not just because her body connected her physically to an abandoned culture but also because of its incorporation of that culture's language. As Murasaki puts it, "You couldn't have a bridge party if you had an immigrant mother who sat muttering beside the door" (97). Kay feels restricted by the cultural message her mother insists on sending. But rather than taking the opportunity for perceived cultural neutrality that Naoe's departure presents her, a supposed relief of the burden of caring for an old woman with increasingly threatening strange behavior, Kay suffers a complete mental breakdown. Naoe's departure does not offer cultural neutrality, and Kay's breakdown symbolizes a fight against her own attempted assimilation.

Murasaki, who has been so carefully protected from Japanese culture with the exception of the "vegetable blind spot" presented by the "Jap oranges," which almost turn her yellow (91–92), understands intuitively how to address the lack that stymies her mother. Obāchan, the happy recipient of mysterious, secret packages of *Osenbei* and sake, laments, before her escape, the rejection of Japanese food that has changed her daughter entirely: "My daughter, you were raised on fish cakes and pickled plums. This Western food has changed you and you've grown more opaque even as your heart has brittled" (13). Murasaki senses through an imaginary conversation with her escaped grandmother what sustenance her mother needs and begins to fill the cultural gap by learning to cook traditional Japanese food. She provides a connection to the Japanese culture she has only glimpsed in boxes sent from her great-uncle and sneaked upstairs by night. Though still bereft of the language, Murasaki brings back some of the cultural sustenance that stands in figuratively for the influence her grandmother had maintained over the home.

The boundaries between grandmother and granddaughter blur and practically dissolve through the cacophonous narration of *Chorus of Mushrooms*. The final chapters show such a synchronicity of action that it is difficult to tell whether a passage about a man and woman who have sex in a bathtub relates Murasaki's experience or Naoe's. The possibility that Naoe could be sexually desirous and desirable certainly jars readers' expectations (188). When the scene is made clear pages later (readers envision Naoe with "bathwrinkled fingers" sitting with a cigarette-smoking companion), readers fully witness the gradual dissolve between granddaughter and grandmother (193). Readers can confront their assumptions about old women in a way that expands conceptual possibilities.

Naoe and Murasaki's union culminates in Murasaki's temporary inhabitation of Naoe's chair, the old woman's spatial stake prior to her escape. Naoe marks her own territory within the house by making small grooves in a chair with her buttocks. Naoe's chair, her one territorial claim within an otherwise inhospitable house, similarly represents her body in that both are stark and weathered: "It had a flat back with no ornamentation and no armrests to offer meagre comfort. A simple chair with only a hint of a concave the old woman's buttocks had worn away over two decades of perseverance" (166–67). Described as an "extension of [her] body," Naoe's chair becomes a refuge, a stronghold (housing her as "sentinel" or "protectress" [175]), and eventually a possible hindrance to her freedom (14): "The chair had lent her stability in the midst of prairie dust and wind, but she could easily let it become her prison" (80). Speaking of "my chair of incubation," Naoe decides, "I must leave this chair like a husk, leave like a newly formed cicada" (77). In order to flee, Naoe needs to free herself from the only physical object with which she identifies, so she metaphorically transforms the chair into a body part she must leave behind (signaling a new stage of development in her release from a cocoon rather than the typically expected end of her life). The transformation she brings about is so effective that the chair itself becomes the vehicle of transformation and in turn conveys cultural knowledge, specifically Japanese words, to Murasaki. It is by means of that cultural knowledge that the imaginary connection continues.

The multivocal narration of this novel intensifies and symbolizes the ultimate connection of old and young. Naoe becomes a rodeo star. Read literally, Goto's depiction of Naoe suggests that alternate possibilities of living old include becoming an octogenarian rodeo star. Read figuratively, Goto's Naoe makes possible a similar realm of seeming impossibility. Old women could be considered powerful within language; old women could be valued culturally and socially; old women could maintain control over their destiny. Goto's freeing metaphors provide a refreshing counterpoint to the damage more common metaphors do to perceptions of old age, so that old women are no longer old birds, bats, or shrews. Deliberately making Naoe's experience into a metaphor—Naoe is a rodeo star—forces a recognition of a liberatory potential nestled within figurative language. Because of the connection between a grandmother and a granddaughter, the old bird becomes a freed cicada, a plumped-up chicken, and an extremely sexual rodeo star.

Chorus of Mushrooms confronts readers with their expectations about old age, so that they have to adjust what they imagine to be (im)possible in order to understand the complex layering of narrative voices. In the process Goto makes crucial all three female generations, so that the intergenerational struggles provide the connection between grandmother and granddaughter with the impetus to restore cultural knowledge. Naoe's example inspires Murasaki's adult choice to immerse herself in Japanese culture so much that the novel concludes with Murasaki's open-ended flight to Japan, which reverses Naoe's earlier migration.

The Potential of Grandmotherhood

Collectively, *Duet for Three* and *Chorus of Mushrooms* challenge the supposed dependence implied by moving in with relatives when changes associated with aging prevent living alone. Grandmotherhood can offer old women an opportunity to contribute to and benefit from generation gaps. The physical care they may indeed require when they live with offspring does not have to mark their subsequent ultimate decline and diminishment. Barfoot and Goto pull readers into other possibilities and opportunities, so that both of these novels suggest another way for females to express and share devotion, experience, and story. Because sacrifice and responsibility are not the primary modes by which grandmothers and granddaughters are meant to relate, Frances and Murasaki do not cancel out their grandmothers metaphorically or otherwise. There is such distance between Frances's small town and urban lives that she can attribute the difference between her and Aggie to external factors and appreciate the gains of both shared love and different opportunities. Murasaki and Naoe do not even share a language, and so, despite the embarrassment Murasaki admits to having felt, she can embrace the difference to the extent that her adult life commits itself to bridging the cultural gulf rather than condemning her grandmother for perceived limitations. The relationships forged in each of these novels exceed the potential inherent in mother-daughter conflict because there is no either/or configuration.

A shifted focus from aging bodies to how aging bodies relate to family members moves the crux of late life from physical pain to emotional connection. Grandmotherhood can provide a unique possibility for generosity and mutual love that does not have to entail self-sacrifice or the abandonment of personal goals. Whether living with family or simply relating to them from afar, grandmothers can participate in the new family position, but when they live with family members, the new role is most likely to take precedence over other interpersonal bonds. In concentrating on a future generation, an old woman can evaluate her own experiences and close the gap between self-pity and self-love. Narratives centered on the relationship between grandmother and granddaughter may be able to counter the debilitating mirror gazing I discussed in chapter 2 and opt instead for the matter-of-fact acceptance of self-image hinted at by Goto's metaphors of sound.

Chapter Three

"Here, Every Minute Is Ninety Seconds": Fictional Perspectives on Nursing Home Care

Moving in with relatives because of physical and/or economic needs that accompany late life implies a dependence that looms even larger over the choice to enter an institution. In three of the novels discussed so far, the nursing home threat precipitates the crisis of the narrative. In *The Stone Angel,* the Silverthreads visit causes the central conflict of the novel, especially in terms of its present-tense narrative (Laurence 1964). In *Duet for Three,* Aggie's incontinence causes June finally to investigate the local nursing home on behalf of her mother, and the novel resolves to some degree with Aggie's assent that "I know we'll have to do something" (Barfoot 1985, 248). The threat that June's exploration poses prompts the retrospective narration that makes up much of the plot, motivates the content of the stories told, and makes Frances's upcoming visit crucial to the interactions between the two older women. In *Chorus of Mushrooms,* the ominous Silver Springs Lodge enters Kay's thinking about her mother because she misunderstands the old woman's increasingly strange behavior (Goto 1994). Consequently, Naoe begins her physical journey. Each novel depicts an old woman as reluctant to enter an institution and her offspring in turn as hesitating to commit (as it is so frequently put) a parent to such a place. Each character agonizes over the choice until it can be presented as the only viable option. The situations these novels depict do not necessarily represent either actual decisions about nursing home care or even novelistic depictions of the institutions, but they do potently signify the ominous symbol that the nursing home can be for the elderly and those caring for and about them. Currently, nursing homes signal failure—of old people to remain independent and of family members to provide adequate care. Nursing homes invite fear partly because they house a conglomeration of what people often dread about old age. If old age were not necessarily to conjure up negative opinion, nursing homes may, in turn, not seem or be as threatening.

Housing the Old, Containing Negativity: Two Narrative Examples

The Stone Angel invests heavily in the negative associations that come with nursing home care. Hagar's terror of Silverthreads symbolizes her terror of old age and of being old more generally. Though she rankles against dependence on her offspring, that dependence seems comfortable compared to what Silverthreads menaces. Hagar discovers Marvin and Doris's seemingly treacherous plot when she stumbles upon a brochure in the kitchen, rather than when Marvin and Doris discuss it with her. Similarly, she claims that Marvin and Doris trick her into a visit, and she dramatizes her emotional fragility on the journey to the home: "After supper they baggage me into the car and off we go. I ride in the back seat alone. Bundled around with a packing of puffy pillows, I am held securely like an egg in a crate" (Laurence 1964, 93). The control Hagar maintains over readers' perspectives has a double edge in this metaphoric moment because she both captures the ignominy of being forced to travel against her will and yet reinforces the physical fragility that suggests the necessity of her move.

Hagar's reaction to Silverthreads, after the initial shock of being taken for a visit against her will, is typical of how nursing homes are figured and described culturally. She is dismayed by the anonymity and uniformity conferred upon the inmates. She regrets praising the pane windows because her admiration situates her with the other "unanimous old ewes" (98) who inhabit this "mausoleum" (96). Her attempt to refuse the stifling category of old age is threatened when she inadvertently adopts behaviors of the residents. Accordingly, a passing nurse elides her with other inmates: "A young high-bosomed nurse flips open the main door, nods without seeing me, crosses the porch, goes out and down the steps" (99). The devastating possibility that she may blend in with all of the others terrifies Hagar to the extent that the visit to Silverthreads motivates her final escape attempt (running to the cannery). Through Hagar, Laurence figures Silverthreads as a place where individuality disappears alongside the more obvious loss of independence. That homogeneity typifies the way in which old people relegated (as it is so frequently expressed) to institutions are considered primarily if not solely as old (and therefore dependent).

Hagar undercuts this uniformity, however, by immediately and intricately individuating the various inmates she encounters, thereby variegating the category of old age. She instantly dislikes Miss Tyrrwhit, who "pats at her hair with a claw yellow as a kite's foot" mostly because of the picture she paints of living at Silverthreads (101). Despite her own distaste, Hagar does not wish to face vivid descriptions of the meals and other details of her potential residence. In spite of herself, she is much more amenable to Mrs. Steiner, who fits another stereotype of old women—the photograph wielder. Hagar's conversation with Mrs. Steiner hints at a community strength at Silverthreads that could perhaps offer Hagar something she does not have at her present home. Still, when Mrs. Steiner verbalizes the connection she feels with Hagar and suggests the two of them could benefit from living at Silverthreads together—"'Well, you and I would get on pretty good. . . . I hope we see you here'" (104)—Hagar cannot accept the possibility and contemplates the escape attempt that both actualizes and prevents her eventual participation in a female community similar to the one hinted at in her visit to Silverthreads. The negative associations Hagar makes with old age are writ large at Silverthreads, with the result that she is unable to accept either her age or residency there.

May Sarton's *As We Are Now* (1973) provides another (in this case American) narrative example of negative discourses surrounding nursing homes. Seventy-six-year-old Caro Spencer is literally (if her narration is to be believed) abandoned in a decrepit, dirty facility with inadequate, even abusive caregivers. Miles from other dwellings and badly maintained, the home harbors old people whose families can hardly bear even to visit them any longer. The home also encapsulates countless cultural fears of decrepitude and isolation. When Caro incinerates the building, she explodes negative depictions and treatment of old age from the inside by taking advantage of the very attitudes that assume her incapacity and cause such treatment. Read literally, *As We Are Now* presents serious concerns about the abuse of old people in institutional care; read figuratively, the novel localizes fears of age and provides the elderly the tools with which to dismantle such fears.

Caro tells readers that when she defies her caregivers, she is placed in a dark room for days at a time. It is difficult to discern the accuracy of her story because she depicts her wardens' description of her as demented and she reports that all of the inmates are drugged, either of which could be the case. As Barbara Frey Waxman explains, "Sarton may want Caro's text to enable readers to experience an elderly person's lapses into mental confusion and anxiety about the unreliability of her own senses in perceiving reality. Experiencing such sensations through Caro's journal may be a young or middle-aged reader's ticket into the foreign country of senescence" (1990, 142). Because the caregivers never provide their version, readers must determine who is trustworthy. She may be demented, she may be drugged, but Caro's experience nevertheless is clearly agonizing. She tells readers, "I am in a concentration camp for the old, a place where people dump their parents or relatives exactly as though it were an ash can" (Sarton 1973, 9). The journal form of the novel embodies Caro's attempts to maintain clarity of mind. As she writes, "This document is becoming in a very real sense my stay against confusion of the mind. When I feel my mind slipping, I go back and rediscover what really happened" (69). While she sadly discourages herself from hope, which she claims damages more than any other emotion, she struggles to come to terms with her old age and its signification. The only way for Caro to take agency is to destroy the home, literalizing her exaggerated concentration camp claim. To do so, she takes advantage of assumptions of the unreliability and incapacity of the old. She starts the fatal fire, making it look as though the blaze is caused by the carelessness that others expect of someone her age, despite the presumed assumption that an old person could not be capable of such an action.

As We Are Now puts readers in intimate touch with the emotions that can accompany professional care. It is an extreme example because the home clearly houses, or at least is depicted by Caro as housing, abuse. This is not the shiny faceless institution featured in news items; this is the embodiment of metaphoric associations of old age. Full of dirt, meanness, and insanity, the home incorporates cultural detritus for Caro to analyze. When she destroys the home, she acts against the assumptions that have made it possible for her to end up there, drawing on those very assumptions in order to do so. One hopes that such negative thinking also goes up in smoke. Readers cannot help but sympathize with Caro, especially because Sarton depicts touchstone characters, such as Reverend Thornhill, as agreeing with Caro's agony and attempting to alleviate it. She gives Caro the power to act against her own situation. Though perhaps a bit simplistic, *As We Are Now* at the very least allows readers to witness and deplore both nursing home abuse and the attitudes that generate such treatment.

Theorizing the Nursing Home

As these novels' depictions illustrate, it is extremely difficult to theorize the nursing home. So much depends not only on cultural but also on geographical considerations. Because of vast differences in health care funding, for example, dilemmas differ drastically for Americans and

Canadians when they consider moving themselves or their parents into institutional care. The issue becomes politically charged because there is such a vast difference between public and private institutions. As a result, individual economic choices enter into any such decision and change the emphasis of the emotional consequences. Even more than these to some degree generalizable differences, there are countless factors—health, mobility, habits, age, sex, mental acuity—in each individual case that make any theoretical conclusions about nursing homes inevitably reproduce the institutions' own biggest flaw: a tendency to homogenize the very old. In *The Stone Angel* and *As We Are Now,* the treatment of institutional care both enacts and criticizes that tendency. As with most aspects of old age, nursing home life demands a continued consideration of the physical aspects of changing age, especially because relatives and medical practitioners usually cite physical infirmity as the trigger for the decision. Caregivers face the intricate difficulty of emphasizing individuals without overprivileging the physical demise old age is too often thought to be. Fiction faces a similar problem, though the results of either choice are of course less dire in an immediate sense. Whereas *The Stone Angel* and *As We Are Now* forcefully emphasize the physical dimensions of what Hagar and Caro perceive as indignity, later works—discussed in this chapter—also draw on caregivers' perspectives to broaden their depictions of institutional care.

"The Nursing Home Specter"

In *The Fountain of Age (*1993), Betty Friedan's chapter title "The Nursing Home Specter" captures the ways in which care facilities permeate popular thinking about old age without adequate, concrete elaboration. A number of popular works, geared toward a general audience, take on nursing home care and its haunting legacy from the Victorian poorhouse. Julietta K. Arthur, in her 1954 *How to Help Older People: A Guide for You and Your Family,* explicitly but unconvincingly addresses homogeneity as a positive aspect of nursing home care. Arthur explains that facilities try to group together people they predict will get along based on similar backgrounds. Her explanation is pragmatic: "This is not snobbishness. It is a practical recognition that problems arise when people live together whose life patterns were set long before they met each other. Homogeneity helps to eliminate sources of possible friction" (241). Although dated, this reasoning at least shows an attempt to recognize individual similarities, acknowledging that old people have distinct backgrounds that can be matched. Accordingly, there are differences among the elderly, but there are distinct groups within which members can be considered alike. However, the underlying assumption, oddly, is that people with similar experiences will experience old age similarly. By emphasizing experiences, Arthur eschews the dangerous overconsideration of physical change and even avoids merely grouping together those with similar physical challenges. She considers similar experience to be more significant than myriad other similarities or differences. An even larger problem occurs when the similarity of being old is thought to be greater than other potential similarities and differences, however constructive or complicating. It is dangerous to think of old age as an overreaching, uniform category rather than as a descriptive term that might apply to a large number of distinct people with different needs, experiences, and expectations. To perceive age first supports the melding of individual differences that, necessarily to some degree, governs many institutions.

Because old age is so frequently thought of as a unifying similarity and because nursing homes are usually populated with old people, nursing homes themselves face countless stereotypes that challenge their own distinctness. Judging from media coverage, medical textbooks, and many fictional depictions, a typical understanding of a nursing home includes physical restraints, forced confinement, being committed against one's will, overmedication, diapers, bad food, and a general lapse into an undesirable complete dependence. Often people fear that moving into a place designated for old people will confirm age as a defining characteristic and that the most negative physical changes imaginable will accompany that designation. Numerous media reports about nursing homes support a general understanding of such places as repositories of dependence and abuse. Typical images accompanying such coverage consist of an elderly resident lying helplessly in bed with some other younger human figure, a relative or employee, standing nearby in order to provide a contrast that emphasizes the "plight" of the elderly. A series of fires in Montreal nursing homes raised compelling questions because of repeated disturbing images of elderly patients clothed only in diapers carried out into cold weather. Such images support the prevailing negative associations that nursing homes provoke. However, such treatment—not adequately dressing those residents who require help—surely constitutes an abuse of a system that does not have to treat the elderly people, upon whom it wholly relies, as invalid.

Friedan cites many American institutions where residents are physically restrained and neglected. To heighten her point, she invokes personal experience to condemn institutional care: "In ten years of research, no data has emerged to counteract my impression of nursing homes as death sentences, the final interment [*sic*] from which there is no exit but death. . . . Of 'no apparent cause,' as they said of my mother.

She died in her sleep 'of old age'; she was ninety. I think she had no wish to live any longer, in that nursing home; no bonds, no people she cared about, no purpose to her days" (1993, 510). Friedan's experience is, however unfortunately, not at all unique. She goes on to cite numerous instances where physical and mental deterioration, even to the point of death, increase when older adults find themselves in nursing homes that restrict freedom of choice or personal control. The overriding and most damaging process of the negative associations with nursing homes is the development of dependency or even just an attitude of dependency to the extent that individuals lose control or distinction.

Not surprisingly, analysts of nursing home care continually cite, as I have, the tendency to generalize and not treat elderly people (sometimes referred to as inmates, residents, patients, or, if lucky, consumers) as individuals. In contrast to her poignant description of how institutional care contributed to her mother's death, Friedan offers positive examples of alternate models for group care that continually provide residents with choices that individuate them and counter their perceived dependency. The California Live Oaks Living Center and numerous group homes in Oregon cluster their caregiving strategies around the individual desires of the old people they house. For example, residents are free to move back and forth between acute care and supported living, with the result that any one resident's physical situation does not define that person within his or her living space. In her discussion of "the dignity of risk," Clara Pratt (director of Oregon State University's gerontology program) unconsciously echoes William F. Forbes, Jennifer A. Jackson, and Arthur S. Kraus's explanation of the importance of allowing old people to take risks: "[T]he need for an individual's independence and privacy makes it necessary to accept some risks, including the possibility of falls" (quoted in Friedan, 528; Forbes, Jackson, and Kraus 1987, 74). Because of a seeming need to characterize the very old as feeble in order to maintain a comfortable distance perhaps from younger bodies, caregivers sometimes become overly protective. (A narrative example of this would be Hagar Shipley's feeling trapped like an egg in a crate.) Protectiveness is not always a productive mind-set for helping an elderly person decide to enter an institution. Understanding the need for continued life, rather than living in fear of risk, helps nursing home residents to develop a fulfilling community in late life. As Friedan describes them, the potential results of an alternate model at Live Oaks are remarkable in terms of physical rehabilitation and the general well-being of residents.

Clearly, the negative associations that govern cultural attitudes toward late-life institutional care need to be changed. As Friedan points out, this can be a matter of life and death. The poor popular image of nursing homes likely results from both actuality and normative myth (similar to the Japanese lazy housewife narrative that Margaret Lock describes). Forbes, Jackson, and Kraus, citing the Victorian poorhouse model, blame unfit decisions and common attitudes about the hopelessness of nursing home stays for the negative public opinion (1987, xi). As much as I would like it to be otherwise, I sincerely doubt that literature will affect funding for nursing home care. The problem is as large as the healthcare system and appears hopeless for those old people without the means to pay exorbitantly for "luxury" care. It is, however, possible that literary depictions of old people in general, and of institutions specifically, might generate critical thought and debate. They might also incite residents to come to grips with both the changes their aging entails and the ones it does not necessarily entail.

When I visited a friend's grandmother in an Ontario care facility, I was struck by how my idealism was a far cry from the actuality of the situation before me. Because of strain on the system and a lack of personal funds for a nearby private facility, the resident had been placed in an institution an hour away from her family rather than within walking distance. Notes about the previous occupant of her bed remained at its head, with the result that staff could easily confuse her name and dietary requirements. As we chatted in the common room, I was overwhelmed by her new reckoning with age identity. She told us that "we old people" are different, and she struggled to understand how that difference worked. Perhaps, in addition to the prevalent fashion shows and carol singing, a reading group that focused on novels about aging could promote discussion about the new identity she was taking on.

After that experience, in the interest of volunteering in local seniors' residences, I attended an orientation session for the Vancouver Regional Health Board's Volunteers for Seniors program. The main goal seemed to be an assessment of whether potential volunteers (I was the only one in attendance) would be able to stomach the nursing home scenario. To ensure that I made an informed decision, the organizer screened the Canadian National Film Board's (NFB) production devastatingly titled *Priory: The Only Home I've Got.* The orientation leader assured me that the film was made in the 1990s, but in fact it was released in 1978. The opening shot shows a woman delicately transported, wrapped in a blanket, from a vehicle into an institution. Viewers gradually learn that this woman has just been placed in Priory, and she is not at all happy with that decision. She refuses to eat and appears generally bewildered throughout the documentary. Of course, her discomfort may come not only from being forced into an institution that she may not have chosen, but also, or even more, from having that painful moment intruded upon not only by a host of caregivers but also by a camera crew. It is possible that a greater good may have occurred from the intrusion because the film provides what seems to be a thorough and balanced glimpse of institutional life for the elderly. Still, I suspect one individual's dignity need not have been sacrificed for that accomplishment.

The NFB makes nursing home life a subject for close scrutiny in their 1970s' production. For the most part they do so without exploiting the elderly charges. They provide even coverage of the humor and pain of living in such an institution, with an emphasis on activities designed to make residents feel they participate in a larger social world. They show nursing home residents swimming, wrapping Christmas presents, dancing, and talking in groups in addition to more clichéd depictions of crying and confused nighttime behavior. Viewers can assume some knowledge of nursing home life from engaging with the film and may even understand the particularities of aging in the process. Still, the filmmakers do not really provide an inclusive view. There is no real sense of inside knowledge or understanding. Instead viewers are situated with volunteers and caregivers who go into the home and try to engage with the funny and pathetic residents. A strong barrier between "us" (younger) and "them" (older) remains.

In a move away from traditional documentaries, codirector Owen Kydd calls his film *You Are Here* (winner of the 1998 Montreal Film Festival in the category of best student documentary), a "poetic documentary, comparing two buildings" (personal interview, December 28, 1998). In the process of comparing a functioning nursing home, occupied by residents, with a defunct one, occupied by squatters, the video juxtaposes two conversations. The piece begins in a Vancouver nursing home where female residents gather in a discussion group clearly carefully designed for their own personal expression. They discuss contemporary and past issues, as well as life in the nursing home. Presumably expressing her frustration with nursing home staff, one woman jeers, "I'll be back in a minute. Here, every minute is ninety seconds." Viewers are situated as participants (although they are listeners) in the conversation. A contrasting conversation occurs among young squatters in a café where the men and women discuss the strategy behind their future occupation of the defunct building. They excitedly contemplate the possibilities of what could still be inside the former institution. The juxtaposition not only provides viewers many vantage points from which to imagine nursing home space, it also gives the old women power of possession and the nursing home potential for transgressive excitement. The nursing home specter can be debunked only if care for the elderly in institutions changes. Nursing home reform depends on agitation not only from without but also from within the system.

The Role of the Caregiver

The caregiver's perspective on nursing home care and on nursing home reform is crucial. I have discussed elsewhere the role that family members, and especially female family members, play in caring for elderly relatives. This chapter examines the role of professional caregivers in the establishment of and challenges to current problems in nursing home care. Current gerontological nursing textbooks sometimes stress the importance of individuating care for the elderly and thus occasionally avoid and even combat the pervasive homogenization of late-life care. A recent study suggests that caregivers themselves need to operate as individuals in order to have a larger, systematic effect within their profession (Dimond 1996, 14). Because nurses are responsible for physical care, they require an elaborate understanding of chronic illnesses. The crucial differentiation among residents can begin here, at a physical level. Beyond physical needs, the recognition of their own potential individual roles can then lead nurses to understand and partake of the necessary steps toward new understandings of autonomy within nursing homes (Aller and Van Ess Coeling 1996, 22). Having nurses participate in the choice residents make to enter a nursing home makes them aware of the lives outside that differentiate residents on the basis of past experiences (Bliesmer and Earle 1996, 35).

Loretta Aller and Harriet Van Ess Coeling's "Quality of Life from the Long-Term Care Resident's Perspective" is not, as one would expect from its title, written by residents but rather by health care professionals. The article evaluates the difference between what caregivers perceive to be important indicators of quality of life for elderly residents and what elderly residents claim in interviews are actual indicators. Current research by professionals in the field claims that "physical environment, recreational activities, and social environment" are key factors to long-term care quality of life (1996, 21). In fact, residents identify only the latter as crucial, and they do so only insofar as they stress the importance of social interaction: "'I've made a lot of friends since I've been here.' Other typical comments: 'I like to meet people' and 'People are the most important thing'" (20). When actually consulted (spoken with), residents pinpoint communication as a priority for improving the quality of life in an institution. Such communication presumably involves not just exchanges of seemingly vital information but also narrative discussions.

Forbes, Jackson, and Kraus stress communicative strategies between caregivers and residents as crucial to the development of individualized care. They explain a method for addressing problems of mental disorientation commonly associated with the elderly, a technique intriguingly named "reality orientation": "The technique uses a process of day-to-day information exchanges between staff and resident that aims to stimulate and develop the senses and to increase social contacts. This provides support to the individual's failing memory and a feeling of comfort and security to the confused. A sense of security, a steady supportive relationship with staff and a reduction in the level of anxiety may also have a beneficial effect on memory and behaviour" (1987, 75–76). Caregivers deliberately speak directly with residents about the choices to be made and try to value personal knowledge of their increasingly confined world. The idea is that this strategy orients residents to a "reality" that has perhaps been forced upon them. That such a process must be named and encouraged is sad testimony to the assumptions made, even (or especially) within the medical discipline dedicated to their care. The key to the "reality orientation" solution is communication with individual residents to create a shared understanding of what constitutes a shared "reality" and not simply to assume that understanding without dialogue.

Gail Landau, a healthcare worker in a Toronto nursing home, writes of attention to entire individual care in a poignant 1998 *Globe and Mail* article. She emphasizes the familiarity that allows her to see beyond the age of the residents to their individuality. In contrast with the general public to whom she writes, Landau explains, "Mrs. L. does not look to us like Y. Simply because they are both small, old and grey." She explains how seemingly small details become individualized rituals with each resident and that "establishing the appropriate relationship with the residents is part of the task." She touches on the displeasure that forcing a resident to wash against his will gives the three caregivers it requires and does not ignore other negative aspects of her job: "stress-related tempers, suspicious family members, unrealistic regulations." But she goes a long way to debunk numerous erroneous assumptions and even describes mealtime as an exciting individualized moment when caregivers scramble to meet the distinct desires and tastes of the one hundred and fifty residents. For Landau, experience has eliminated the troubling views she had about elderly people when she trained: "On my break, my mind returns to the nursing home where I trained. My first impression was that it was dark, with a pervasive smell of 'oldness.' Fragile bodies, pale faces. Unanswered calls for help. Now I wonder at how those impressions have evaporated. Warmth and familiarity have replaced the darkness." Landau relates her experience in the hope that she can pass on her increased understanding through illustrations of the people she knows. She writes a personal narrative that offers a similar opportunity to a general public because they can share in a new understanding of the individuals where she works and thus potentially transform their attitudes alongside hers. Her piece suggests that narrative is an important mode for organizing and relating the processes of change necessary to nursing home care, as well as for making an appeal to a general public whose attitudes must also change in order for reforms to succeed.

The gerontological texts cited thus far touch on gerontological strategies, such as "reality orientation," to create a better understanding, by younger people, of old people in nursing homes. The intended audience of those texts comprises healthcare professionals and gerontological researchers, so the appeal is specific and limited. Landau's newspaper item appeals to a larger audience, but does so directly in connection to personal experience in the hope of stimulating selfish interest on the part of readers. I suggest that narrative fiction offers a richer venue for bridging the gap between elderly people and younger people—maybe even for providing a "reality orientation" in the sense of dialogism more than actual concrete lived experience. The texts seem to offer data for research about nursing homes, but more so they theorize institutions in such a way as to make abstract claims about the homes' as yet largely unfulfilled possibilities for companionship, mutual support, and change.

Narrating the Nursing Home: Edna Alford's *A Sleep Full of Dreams*

Two works of fiction I discuss in detail in this chapter situate relationships between young caregivers and older nursing home residents in an institutional setting and offer readers at least dual, though perhaps pretending to be neutral, access into long-term care in Canadian and West Indian settings. Through third-person descriptions of common space, Edna Alford, in *A Sleep Full of Dreams* (1981), manages to draw readers inside an institution in a way the nonfiction texts I have cited cannot. Readers participate in the disturbing disjunction that the homogenization of individuals causes and must follow the main character to negotiate the attendant complications. That character, Arla, acts as a cipher for what readers have to do in connection with narrative fiction. Shani Mootoo, in *Cereus Blooms at Night* (1996), adopts a first-person voice through a character not usual to contemporary fiction and thus pretends to possess a personal insight to which most readers will need to adjust: evaluating old age in an institution by means of a transvestite body and mind. These caregiver figures are especially interesting because of the theory of readership they offer allegorically.

In Edna Alford's collection, the short stories are linked by their setting in a Calgary nursing home, Pine Mountain Lodge, and by the character of Arla, a young, female caregiver who works with the elderly characters in each vignette. Although Alford writes in the third person, Arla's continued presence encourages the reader to evaluate and relate to her constantly changing and developing perceptions of the older adults she attends. Arla's assumptions are continually undermined, whether she begins a story with a negative opinion that some new knowledge thwarts or starts out full of optimism that is debunked. Accordingly, readers can accompany Arla through this third-person, partially omniscient narration in her continual reevaluation of her job, Pine Mountain Lodge's residents, and her own thoughts on aging. Alford subtly and gradually alters the seeming neutrality that the third person sets up by introducing various Pine Mountain residents.

Overall there is a stark disjunction, reflected architecturally, within the nursing home. The contrast between the individual stories of the characters as located in their personal rooms and their uniformity in the dining room and common areas crystallizes the conflict between homogeneity and individuality that inhabits the institutional setting of any nursing home. Via their settings, the stories manage to evoke what the gerontological nursing textbooks begin to hint at—that individuality is crucial to an overall interaction with aging residents. The difference Friedan illuminates between certain institutions and the Live Oaks Living Center is accomplished and elaborated in Alford's depiction of an unenlivened, typical, institutional setting. The dining room, especially, flattens the individual characterizations of residents that occur throughout the rest of the stories, set elsewhere.

The first story of the collection, "The Hoyer," comments on the nature of representation and storytelling between generations. Arla takes Miss Bole from her room, where her own art work differentiates her as a valuable citizen who contributed greatly to a larger community, to a general bathing room, where she is just another old, incapacitated body. Arla hoists her into the room on a machine that further dehumanizes the processes that continue to maintain her body in old age. As revenge for the fear invoked by this instrument, Miss Bole repeatedly tells grotesque and grim stories of farm accidents to Arla. She seems to hope that the young woman will be so shaken that she will err in the bath-giving process and justify both the old woman's fear and possibly even a change in procedure.

At a point when the hoyer severely restricts Miss Bole's mobility, she turns to the only site of power remaining to her: her ability to tell stories based on a vast and disturbing set of experiences. The resulting disguised battle conceals the women's acute awareness of each other. Miss Bole knows the limits of her game: "[S]he always tested only as far as she safely could, never far enough to push the girl over the edge into anger because that was very dangerous" (10). She is also fully aware of the effect she produces but plays on conceptions of an elderly, unreliable mind to achieve the desired results: "'I don't b'lieve I ever told you 'bout the time I's at my cousin's place.' They both knew she had and both knew that the other knew" (15). Miss Bole tells stories and weaves narratives to evoke in Arla the fear she herself repeatedly feels at the young woman's hands. The patterns of her repeated tales affect Arla, allowing readers to understand the power that fictionalized narrative (the stories seem to have some basis in Miss Bole's past) can have. In this depiction, old people's stories are meant to disturb, and readers are offered in Arla a touchstone for a typical, likely familiar reaction to the usually irritating, repetitive narratives of the old.

When the two return to Miss Bole's room, a department of cultural affairs representative awaits the old woman because she has an interest in Miss Bole's earlier artistic production. Arla inquires into the type of paintings, which she has never taken seriously—old people's stories are not to be fully credited after all. Lyanda Weatherby tells her that "'most of them are of meadows filled with flowers so perfectly executed and flawless that for a long time the critics didn't consider them seriously at all'" (26). The exact mimicry of the repeated gruesome stories is replicated, with starkly different subject matter, in the paintings that have garnered the woman's fame. Both try accurately and repeatedly to depict an external actuality. The contrast between the pictures' idyllic and the stories' gruesome subject matter leads the reader to wonder what rebellion the old woman's art may enact. Having followed Arla as an exemplary interpreter of old people and sensed her error in failing to comprehend the significance of Miss Bole's ruthless replication, readers reevaluate both the stories of the old and the interpretations Arla offers.

The following story, "Mid-May's Eldest Child," reverses the pattern of "The Hoyer" in that Arla approaches Miss Moss looking forward to her impending interaction with the old woman. Her plans to thwart nursing home policy in a day away from Pine Mountain excite her because she thinks her plans match Miss Moss's desires. Thinking she understands Miss Moss's love for Romantic poetry, Arla is certain that a connection to the natural world will appeal to the old woman. She distinguishes Miss Moss from other lodge residents and likes her even though other employees consider her "an irascible, uncompromising old witch and they would have as little to do with her as possible unless she mended her ways" (29). Arla is shocked and disappointed by Miss Moss's transformation from the resident "full of spit and fire" and with unequalled rhetoric to a tired, confused, wheezing, old woman in public (29). Again Arla fails to interpret appropriately the individuality of the old people with whom she works. In this case a compulsive optimism and desire to see more than is there fails her and readers. "The Hoyer" suggests that old people have inherently valuable insight to offer younger generations, but "Mid-May's Eldest Child" drastically undercuts this when Miss Moss turns out to need exactly the kind of care and protection the institution offers her.

Their failed outing ends in utter disagreement with Miss Moss threatening to report Arla's flaunting of Pine Mountain Lodge regulations, regulations that Arla mistakenly thought Miss Moss would resent. As a result Arla thinks of Miss Moss as similar to the other residents, in contrast to how the ending of "The Hoyer" leads Arla to an understanding of Miss Bole as unique. Disappointed by the old woman's inability to commune with nature as Arla had envisioned, "Arla began to feel not so much hurt any longer, but anger toward the old woman, she felt herself withdraw, felt the old woman's power over her diminish, was relieved to find herself objective. Miss Moss was just an old woman. That's all she was" (39). Arla's fluctuating between individualizing and generalizing the nursing home residents operates as a metaphor for a cultural necessity to interpret the elderly as complete entities. Arla's conclusion, that Miss Moss is "just an old woman," is clearly insufficient because it has already been proven in the previous story to have no inherent meaning; there is no such thing as "just an *old* woman" any more than feminists at the very least would agree that there is no such thing as "just a woman." Readers become increasingly aware of Arla's futile struggle to maintain a consistent outlook as a caregiver to institutionalized, elderly people. Both the individualities and the similarities of the residents necessitate continual adjustments. Readers learn firsthand the need for such adaptation and develop strategies for understanding and coping with the problems of Pine Mountain Lodge's rules that restrict residents (such as limited outings) alongside Arla.

When Miss Moss vomits at the entry of the lodge steps, Arla remembers what Miss Moss had taught with intense irony. The failure of Romanticism to translate into a gratifying escape to an outside world culminates in Arla's accompaniment to Miss Moss's dry heaves: "'A thing of beauty is a joy forever,' she recited to herself, her voice mocking the old woman's, her mouth twisted, her eyes glazed with anger—'Its loveliness increases; it will never/Pass into nothingness; but still will keep/A bower quiet for use and a sleep/full of sweet dreams and health and quiet breathing'" (40). A sustained one-on-one encounter with the old woman has indeed extended Arla's capacity to interpret the poetry she has learned from the retired teacher. However, the bitterness of failed hopes belies the positive spin Arla repeatedly tries to put on her nursing home job when justifying it to her family and fiancé. Frustratingly,

Arla must continue to understand the many facets of her relationships with various residents and cannot settle on any particular solution to her own, let alone her family's, concerns about her job. At another remove, readers engage with a different textual mode, poetry, and its attempts at representation. Alford derives her title from Keats's lines quoted in this story, with the important elision of the word "sweet," leaving readers to question the nightmare that "the sleep full of dreams" may involve.

In "Fall Cleaning," Alford once again leaves readers in an ambiguous position when a strange lack of empathy on Arla's part thwarts the desperate efforts on the part of Mrs. Tweedsmuir to hoard seemingly useless items, probably so that she can maintain some feeling of control and individual identity. The cleaning of her room has a devastating effect on the old woman, with the result that she requires extra care from Arla. Amidst a flash of insight that Mrs. Tweedsmuir may not have always hoarded junk, Arla nonetheless demonstrates her lack of sympathy: "'If you think that makes you special, Mrs. Tweedsmuir, you're wrong. There's not a woman here who doesn't have something wrong with her but most of them handle it far better than you.' Arla knew she was stretching the truth a little but Mrs. Tweedsmuir was getting on her nerves" (88). While she continues her bitter thoughts, Arla then takes the reader through the excruciatingly slow process of accompanying Mrs. Tweedsmuir to the next room. She begins to adopt the stereotypical attitudes toward aging that she tries to counter in her personal life and that her professional experience should help her to avoid: "She had whiskers growing out of the many moles on her face, like the witches Arla remembered from fairy tales" (89–90). Arla momentarily takes refuge from some of the unpleasant daily aspects of her job by mimicking, with vitriol, the cultural perceptions of old age that can do so much harm. Readers have developed too complex an understanding thus far in the collection of stories to avoid frustration at being offered only Arla's biased view. Still, they recognize in her their own tendencies to vacillate between a rich new understanding of late life and a narrow, easy ageism.

Plays on Arla's changing perspective continue in "Poll 101," wherein Pine Mountain employees, including Arla, encourage Mrs. Bjourensen to vote on the premise that a negligent son awaits her in the voting room. The story ends with Arla's staring at a newspaper page: "She must have figured it was Olaf, Arla thought, and stared at the picture for a long time, long enough to lose herself in the millions of minute black dots on the surface of the newsprint" (107). Arla momentarily avoids the unpleasant realization that she is complicit in the nursing home's deception of Mrs. Bjourensen. She loses herself in the baffling surface array of seemingly meaningless patterned print to slow the process of understanding what lies behind the false image. Similarly, a focus on Mrs. Tweedsmuir's physical match to prevailing notions of typical elderly decay, as is the case with Mrs. Moss, enables Arla to justify a callousness that does not come easily to her because she works one-on-one with nursing home residents daily.

In "Tuesday, Wednesday, Thursday" Arla begins to internalize and identify with the most devastating aspects of nursing home residency to an extent that limits her tenure at the home. Her encounters with the stubborn Mrs. Langland and her resulting impatience end in the stubborn older woman lying in a pool of her own excrement. Alford once again imparts to readers a disgust that exceeds the stereotypical disgust of older bodies that younger people often associate with the elderly. Stereotypically, wrinkles or gray hair may seem worthy of disdain, but what Arla presents in the following is unquestionably vile: "Her face looked like a blank sheet of paper, her eyes large, almost silver, mirroring the eyes of the old woman lying on the floor. The longer Arla stared obliquely at the body, the more she recognized or remembered something familiar in the old woman's frozen face, something unholy in the humiliating posture of the crooked old bone body, framed in the yellow ooze of its own feces" (114). Arla begins to see herself in the helplessness she perceives and struggles to overcome her frustrations and administer the care Mrs. Langland appears to need. Because Arla is unable to maintain her distance, her identification with Mrs. Langland, a recognition that this too could be her own fate, initially pushes her frighteningly closer to damaging attitudes toward elderly flesh: "And although she would never really know why, it tore like a ragged fish-knife through the flesh of her indifference, her only ally at times like this, left her with a deeper repugnance, a more palpable fear and disgust than she had ever felt before, even at Pine Mountain Lodge" (115). Motivated by the association of her own potential plight with that of Mrs. Langland, she tries to overcome this disgust and to offer comfort, with the only response coming from another nursing home resident, Mrs. Mackenzie, who makes clear to Arla that others observe her interactions and either sympathize or disapprove. Arla must reevaluate Mrs. Langland's behavior, defend it to Mrs. Mackenzie, and eventually accept the extent to which it is the potential fate of anyone. Yet, in order to continue in her role at the home and to accept its institutionalized indifference, she simultaneously backgrounds and foregrounds her understanding: "Angry now, forgetting grew easy for her, understanding impossible—both finally of the same thing—that these could be her feet, her toes, her somewhere, some other distant time" (121). To maintain the indifference necessary to represent the institutional setting, Arla continues to force herself to perceive the old people she cares for as similar to her and merely old.

In the final story of the collection, "Companionship," however, Arla faces the impossibility of homogenizing the old women with whom she works. Mrs. Dawson, so nearly a centenarian, after having fallen, cannot survive partly because she is mistreated through indifference similar to that which Arla has attempted to cultivate. As a result, Arla confronts the difficulties of working within the institutional framework at Pine Mountain and can accept its limits no longer. Watching a woman she grew to respect let go of a will to live she knows, from frequent contact, was hard earned, Arla can no longer pretend to maintain the distance she desired: "By now Arla was stooped over the bed, her hands softly cupping the old woman's face, looking hard at the eyes, desperately trying to reach into that space which housed the fight, the will the old woman had brought over from the old country and had worked for years like a plough horse in order to get through all she had" (151). Arla walks away from Pine Mountain for the last time, marking not her failure to work with old women but rather the failure of a specific type of institutionalized setting that does not allow for the kind of care Arla would choose to offer, despite her relentless struggles at indifference. Because she worked closely with Mrs. Dawson and conversed with her often, she knows how small a challenge this last bump on the head should be in comparison to countless preceding vicissitudes. Because Pine Mountain does not provide for the type of companionship (aptly the title of the final story) she develops with Mrs. Dawson, she can no longer tolerate its bounds.

The narratives woven together in *A Sleep Full of Dreams* create a new and developing understanding of the experience of aging and, in particular, aging in an institution. They depict Arla as a dedicated caregiver who is committed to personal interaction. Arla's exit at the conclusion of the stories demonstrates the incongruity of her style of caregiving with institutions that misunderstand and homogenize old age. The collection as a whole, even better than the textbooks, illustrates the potential value of new, innovative, and even basic communicative strategies to adequate, nurturing nursing home care. Further, the falsely neutral narrative voice involves readers imaginatively and evaluates preconceptions of both the homes and the people they house. Arla's job is to interpret the needs and desires of nursing home residents; she is a reader herself, and she offers a paradigm of caring, listening, failing, and engaging.

The Nursing Home as Frame: Shani Mootoo's *Cereus Blooms at Night*

Shani Mootoo's *Cereus Blooms at Night* depends, as a novel, so much on a caregiver-nursing home resident relationship that there is no possibility for Tyler, a nurse, to walk away from Miss Mala Ramchandin, his charge. The friendship that develops between the two characters is as crucial to the transmission of the story as it is to the survival of the two characters themselves. Although most of the novel relates the framed story that explains the past that led Miss Ramchandin to Paradise Alms, the slight frame itself, set in the nursing home, is crucial to that story. In his opening explanation, an address to the reader, Nurse Tyler makes explicit the caregiver's role of passing on old people's stories: "Might I add that my own intention, as the relater of this story, is not to bring notice to myself or my own plight" (1996, 3). He clarifies the necessity of story to his charge, because when she is committed to the home, her personal narrative is her only possession. Readers can imagine, from the very beginning, the communication that must have taken place to enable such transmission and the dedication to listening and understanding on his part it must have required.

As the novel unfolds, the devotion required of Nurse Tyler to divine Mala Ramchandin's story emerges. She does not articulate entire words or even make a sound for the first period of her stay. Tyler has not been allowed to care for any of the other residents of Paradise Alms because of his suspected queerness, so he has more time and attention than other caregivers at nursing homes likely do. Nonetheless, his work typifies the kind of transformation that careful, steady attention may bring about when a caregiver focuses on a patient's desire or need to communicate. Tyler realizes that, although he elicits no response, his own words still have a crucial effect: "I became acutely aware of my movements and the subtleties of my tone, which may have been all that communicated with her" (16). Initially he must read Miss Ramchandin's responses in her body, be it the clenched fists that indicate a fighting spirit, or her "defiant stare, pursed lips and deep, slow, calculated breathing," or her first gesture of turning her head to follow with her eyes, or much later her swinging legs, which indicate happiness (17, 19, 23). As Tyler himself puts it, he becomes "accustomed to reading, as if by Braille, her twitches and gasps" (100).

Unlike Braille, however, Mala's alternative communicative strategies reflect both her own and Tyler's capacities. The twitches and movements seem especially designed for Tyler in the way that Braille is adapted for those who feel better than they see, but Mala's physical gestures also meet her own ends. Most significant, she silently resists when she faces the possibility of losing Tyler's exclusive caregiving attention. He has so effectively normalized her for other staff members that they momentarily think they would rather care for her than for the man who perpetually perceives red ants crawling on him. Not even imagining that she does not care, Tyler fears that she does not comprehend him when he communicates the potential change: "That night I mentioned to

Miss Ramchandin that I would not be spending as much time with her in the future. She didn't respond. I returned to my room but kept one ear open all night waiting, expecting, wondering. As the hours passed and there was no commotion I became more and more despondent" (97–98). Miss Ramchandin waits until the next day and performs the insanity that has brought her Nurse Tyler's special care:

> The centre of the room had been made bare. Three dresses, a slip, two nightgowns, panties, four pairs of socks, a pair of shoes, a night potty, brush and soap were neatly lined up along the edges of the room. A roll of toilet paper had been dissected, sheet by sheet, each sheet pinned to the wall. The dresser lay flat on its face in front of the window. The bed frame, balanced on its side, sat on the dresser. It was straddled by the eating table atop which lay the mattress, which itself lay under four drawers, neatly arranged side by side. Two chairs faced each other with their feet symmetrically placed in the drawers. Straddling the two chairs was the stool and in, or rather on the stool sat Miss Ramchandin. (99)

Mala comprehends to the degree that she fully understands her effect on the other nurses at Paradise Alms and exploits their fear in order to maintain her comfortable situation. More than the strange buzzes and moans she begins to verbalize, her defiant piling of furniture, a defensive gesture long engrained because she hid herself from her father's incestuous advances by building a wall of furniture, signals to Tyler her complete understanding and desire for his care.

When Mala finally begins to communicate verbally, Tyler strains to hear and understand her efforts and realizes, from her repeated query, "Where Asha?" that she has a story to tell. He obtains a notebook in which he scrupulously documents every word she attempts, "no matter how erratic her train of thought appear[s] to be" (99). The respect he accords her is well merited because seemingly random references to insects and gramophones turn out to have devastating significance. The tale Tyler unfolds, though partly a love story, is intensely violent and disturbing. Graphic descriptions of incest and beatings form its core, and Miss Ramchandin's twitches and moans take on a new meaning within its turbulent bounds.

The narrative frame that the meeting of Tyler and Miss Ramchandin constitutes partially mitigates the horrifying center of the story. The retrospective narration is difficult subject matter, and it is well screened by the nursing home surroundings. Readers could possibly ascribe the horror to the setting of the narrative frame rather than to the comfortable domestic setting, which the actual violence ruptures. Accordingly, the relationship that forms between Tyler and Miss Ramchandin and his careful attention to all of the details of her attempted communication become as crucial to the brief narrative frame as to the framed narrative. Without Tyler's continued and justified respect, Miss Ramchandin's sounds could easily be dismissed, even by readers, as the ramblings of a deluded, senile, mental patient. Tyler's diligence, however, carefully informs readers that she has a potent story to tell. Readers subsequently cannot fully concur with the opinions of the other nurses at Paradise Alms, even though they may fervently want to align themselves with those women to deny the terror of Mala's past.

Mootoo plays with the concept of the unreliable narrator, providing touchstones that indicate the utter reliability of the source of her incest narrative and the unreliability of interpretation in connection with that source. She filters descriptions of extreme sexual abuse through an old, discredited body. Instead of thereby discrediting the story or dismissing old age as a natural consequence of abuse, she carefully weaves a tale of intergenerational friendship between outcasts. Readers have to identify with both of them and become careful interpreters of visual and verbal clues, as Tyler demonstrates himself to be.

Conclusion

Both Alford and Mootoo position readers so that they have critical insight into the subtle negotiations involved in caring for elderly women who live in nursing homes. In *Sleep Full of Dreams,* the appeal to the reader takes the form of a false neutrality that reveals a lack of social neutrality in connection to the elderly and especially the biases that typically rule nursing home care. Similar to Goto, Alford encourages readers to examine their own attitudes toward old age that they may previously have thought of as givens rather than opinions. As a result, readers can relate to Arla's growing realization that the situation at Pine Mountain is untenable, and they might also imagine other possible strategies that institutions could adopt. Mootoo filters her appeal to readers so carefully that they have to concentrate on how to negotiate the many subject positions she encourages them to evaluate. The negotiations they undertake in order to connect with troubling subject matter mirror Tyler's own negotiations with Mala. Whereas gerontological nursing textbooks stress the importance of communication, they often present it as a secondary concern in a larger discipline dedicated to the physical care of the elderly. Alford and Mootoo make communicative strategies central in their imaginative depictions of nursing home care.

The nursing home does not have to be understood as a venue of incarceration; it is crucial, however, to remember that for many residents a nursing home is a site of imprisonment. Personal relationships that develop within residences might mediate, mitigate, and even ameliorate the problems of professional care. Readers of the fiction I have selected witness a close relationship between caregivers, visitors, and residents that allows old people relegated, or moved, to institutions the opportunity to tell their stories, to provide a window into a dynamic past, and to make their present more dynamic in the process. The interpersonal connections readers find in *A Sleep Full of Dreams* and *Cereus Blooms at Night* form a stark contrast to assumptions about how old people in care are treated and what old people in care have to offer. The contrast fruitfully encompasses a reimagination of the possibilities of what most people think of as a last resort in frail old age.

Chapter Four

"Living Life Seriatim": Friendship and Interdependence in Late-Life Fiction and Semifiction

The notion of autonomy is prevalent in contemporary North America. As Margaret Urban Walker puts it in "Getting Out of Line: Alternatives to Life as a Career," "The image of the fit, energetic, and productive individual who sets himself a course of progressive achievement within the boundaries of society's rules and institutions, and whose orderly life testifies to his self-discipline and individual effort, remains an icon of our culture" (1999, 102). She explains that such a concept is distinctly gendered so that "Autonomy . . . has long been defined concretely in ways at odds with social demands for appropriate feminine behavior in women" (100). Not only is autonomy gendered, it is also aged, so its definition better fits descriptions of young, able men (Rosemarie Garland Thomson's "normates") than it does older women, with or without disabilities. Further, as Robin N. Fiore explains in "Caring for Ourselves: Peer Care in Autonomous Aging," "Autonomy is commonly contrasted with dependence" (1999, 148). Women, and especially elderly women, are thereby cast as dependent.

In the preceding chapters I have discussed many reasons why it might be harmful to consider late life primarily a time of dependence. Counterproductive and debilitating in itself, the misconception that an elderly person can no longer function without constant aid risks devastating physical, mental, and emotional pain. However, Fiore points out that "Twice as many elderly women as elderly men need supportive care to live independently; 14 percent of elderly women are severely disabled—they cannot climb stairs, walk down the road, bathe completely—

compared to 7 percent of elderly men" (245). Also, women frequently outlive men, so the heterosexual living arrangements that were typical to many North Americans (of a certain generation) when under seventy often cease to be viable to those people now in their seventies and eighties. So far I have written about two possible situations for women living old: moving in with family and moving into nursing homes. Each circumstance involves the potential for a key personal relationship, in the first case with grandchildren and in the second with caregivers. Such cross-generational connections could affect cultural notions of aging for a range of people, with the result that not just the elderly but also those who anticipate aging think through the process. However, each risks dependence whereby, as Fiore explains, a person is "subject to the control of others in matters that affect values and purposes constitutive of one's personality" (248). Though it is possible for younger generations to benefit from hosting or caring for an elderly relative or resident, the potential for reciprocity could remain merely potential.

In this final chapter I want to consider the possible role of interdependence among the elderly, and particularly among older women. Fiore explains that "Sociologists suggest that it is not physical dependency per se that is detrimental to the autonomy of care recipients, but the inability or lack of opportunity to reciprocate, leading to perceived power imbalances and excessive feelings of obligation" (254). She advocates peer care as a possible strategy to redistribute power and to avoid the representation of burdensome old age. Even outside of care situations, the possibilities inherent within late-life friendship allow for a mutuality that might be lacking in inter- and cross-generational relationships. Fiore claims, "friendship provides the condition for the possibility of freedom in an age of comprehensive social regulation" (250). Friendship among the elderly, and especially among elderly women who tend to outlive their male peers, calls into question the automatic association of the elderly with dependence and encourages an identity formation that exceeds the standard "old age as burden" formula. Such friendships could include both longstanding connections that have stood the test of time and new bonds that form in part because of shared experiences of aging. Regardless of whether such friendships result in cohabitation—an alternative to the sometimes restrictive possibilities of living with family or living in an institution—they usually at least trouble the pervasive binary opposition between burdensome old age and useful youth and, in doing so, question the cultural and especially literary emphasis on what Margaret Urban Walker and James Lindeman Nelson refer to as "career selves."

Nelson offers an alternate model for living (and, in his essay, dying) old: "[S]eriatim selves" see "life less as an overall unified project and more as a set of fits and starts" (1999, 122). This model, gleaned from Hilde Lindeman Nelson's phrase "living life seriatim," shifts from privileging any one stage of life since there can be great diversity and change presumably at any point. Whereas Walker's "fit, energetic and productive individual" might view his (the concept as Walker explains it is gendered) life as a single arc with an identifiable climax, leaving old age simply as a denouement with room for reflection, a seriatim self might turn to another less wholistic narrative in order to assess personal value. That is, the seriatim self may value a series of connections to other people rather than prizing the progress of life leading to a unified and successful career. This alternate model allows for a revaluation of the elderly without a falsely positive or reductive invocation of serenity, wisdom, and grace.

Living life seriatim allows for a focus on elderly friendship because it encourages a different value on relationships so that, as Nelson puts it, "A seriatim self has escaped, more or less, the ideological pressures, as well as the ideological and material rewards that encourage people to identify themselves with their careers, and hence may live a life both more shaped by contingencies than by the expression of personal agency and more involved in relationships prized intrinsically, not because they are instrumental to achieving the agent's quest" (123–24). Living life seriatim offers a model of friendship that values the interpersonal benefits over any other end goal. That is, rather than an elderly woman leaning on a daughter because she is unable to live alone, by this model the older woman might turn to her next-door neighbor for a ride to the doctor's office, and in return the neighbor may turn to her for advice about buying a new furnace. This model proposes a type of selfhood not unique to late life but particularly salient to a revaluation of those stages of life.

A shift to valuing personal relationships in and of themselves results not only in reciprocity but also, potentially, in a diminished value for action. In seeking "alternate pictures of well-lived and admirable lives, and ones that may be at odds in the concrete with the kind of individuality and autonomy that a certain kind of society elevates as an ideal" (Walker 1999, 97–98), older people might find value in what had previously been labeled obsolescence. Elderly women are more likely than elderly men to choose seriatim selves (and Nelson notes that this is historically specific so that women of my generation may more likely opt for a career self) and so are more likely to reject the action and experience valued within a career model (127). The increasingly constructive narratives of aging published recently build on the notion of seriatim selves and particularly the ways in which personal relationships, and especially friendships among old women, have intrinsic value. In this chapter I discuss two narratives of elderly friendship: Joan Barfoot's novel *Charlotte and Claudia Keeping in Touch* (1994) depicts two women who have been friends throughout their adult lives reuniting as elderly women and together grappling with cultural expectations of action; Cynthia Scott's semidocumentary film, *The Company of Strangers* (1990), depicts eight women who become friends on a journey taken in late life and defy cultural as well as narrative expectations of action. Despite their different genres, the works collectively comment on the possibilities that late-life friendship, especially its narrative depiction, offers to constructive conceptualizations of old age. In both works the characters' willingness to embark on new friendships and living situations at a relatively late stage eschews the "old age as denouement" pattern typical of a career self. Instead, both illustrate the possibility of and potential within living life seriatim.

Female Friendship and Literary Scholarship

A number of feminist scholars have focused upon female friendship, and particularly female friendship as narrative fiction depicts it. Implicitly this work focuses on friendships among younger women, but it is nonetheless relevant to a study of older women. In conventional fiction female friendships most often remain subservient to heterosexual connections. When female characters interact outside of family connections, they do so usually as part of an overall trajectory toward marriage or male achievement. That is, they are married off or sent to work for male characters. Jane Eyre is a well-known example of such a character as are both Catherines from *Wuthering Heights*. In certain unique, though increasingly more prevalent, cases women writers depict female characters interacting solely for the purpose of their connection and without concern for supposedly masculine (i.e., connected to male characters) goals. Jeannette Winterson has created a number of such characters. The latter cases defy the damaging prescriptive embedded in the former and carefully draw the reader into a new possibility for female communities. Of course, female readers may already understand that female friendship is possible, but a narrative model provides a structure for understanding its potency.

In "(E)merging Identities: The Dynamics of Female Friendship in Contemporary Fiction by Women" (1981), Elizabeth Abel hints at a particular relationship between readers and characters when she argues that female friendship can play a crucial role in self-understanding mostly through commonality: Female characters recognize themselves in each other and gain greater self-knowledge through interaction. Judith

Kegan Gardiner, in her "The (US)es of (I)dentity: A Response to Abel on '(E)merging Identities'" (1981), takes issue with perceived narrowness in Abel's conceptualization and suggests that complementarity can be as crucial to female friendship as commonality, with the result that women may work together to complete each other or profit from comprehending each others' differences. The collaboration between these two feminist scholars—consisting of an article by Abel, a response by Gardiner, and a reply from Abel—supports itself in its form. The two thinkers collectively shift feminist thought from mother-daughter paradigms to other female-female dynamics. Together, Abel and Gardiner develop a model for studying female friendship, and that model can help clarify friendships as novels about groups of old women depict them.

Gardiner explicitly raises the question of how literature, and especially the construction of the characters Abel discusses, affects an analysis of female friendship. She proposes that character criticism such as Abel's psychoanalytic approach can restrict the analysis of social context, and so she stresses the "specifically fictional dimension of the characters" Abel has discussed (437). For Gardiner, fictionality is important because of how fiction comments upon a social world. By examining the fictional elements of the friendships Abel discusses, Gardiner demonstrates that readers can glean crucial insights into a social world, outside fiction. As participants in that social world, readers participate in determining how fiction can fit into an even broader social milieu.

In *Woman to Woman: Female Friendship in Victorian Fiction,* Tess Coslett, directly in dialogue with Abel and implicitly supportive of Gardiner's criticism, discusses fiction's possible role: "Abel's approach here seems to me to be mistaken (and representative of much feminist criticism), in assuming that fiction can and does simply represent 'actuality,' and in assuming that 'narrative considerations' are obstacles to this task. Fiction, I would say, actually *consists* in narrative devices and conventions, and these reflect, embody or even create *not* 'reality' or 'experience,' but ideology" (1988, 2). Coslett claims that in the interstices of literary production lie subtle understandings of a larger social world. Similar to Bakhtin, she implies that fiction offers a type of knowledge but not a reflection of actuality. For Coslett, the structure of fiction—its "narrative devices and conventions"—not only absorbs and repeats prevailing ideology but also prescribes it. Her contribution suggests that literary production and literary study have a potentially vast cultural influence.

For Coslett, narrative fiction is paramount because its conventions could exclude the types of depictions of female friendship crucial to Abel's formulation: "Here, I think, the important point is what is considered as suitable material for a *narrative* as opposed to a letter: what counts as an event in a story. The world of women's friendships seems to be perceived as something *static,* outside the action that makes a story" (11). As Nelson suggests, narratives typically require action, so depictions of female-female friendship can be controlled by popular understandings of both what women are meant to do (or, more often, not to do) and what fiction is meant to encompass. Old women's stories and old women's friendships could also be dynamic narrative happenings, whether or not they match typical expectations of action, that is, whether or not elderly female characters reject "career lives." Rather than being "outside the action that makes a story" and therefore static, these friendships can be outside the action and still make a story. These constructive narratives of aging are based on what Constance Rooke has called a "new paradigm of hope" and grounded in "living life seriatim."

Similar to Nelson's claim about the intrinsic worth of relationships to the seriatim self, Abel explains in a footnote that "while male relationships tend to be more instrumental, oriented toward purposive group activity rather than intimate verbal sharing," "female friendships are emotionally deeper and involve a higher level of self-disclosure" (1981, 415 n. 4). Along with Coslett, I want to explore how depictions of female friendships in fiction present richer possibilities for this multifaceted interpersonal connection than those offered in other media. If narrative fiction taps into a constructed and imaginary world that can reflect and especially affect circulating social thought, then it might also participate in the larger process of rearranging crucial social configurations such as groups of old women, at least in the cultural imagination.

The Possibility of Late-Life Friendship: Contemporary Narrative Examples

There is a hint of late-life friendship in *The Stone Angel.* Hagar catches the first glimmer of female interaction as a possible respite at Silverthreads. Sadly, her interaction with Mrs. Steiner, and its hint at the possibilities that groups of old women offer, actually prompts her fatal escape attempt. Hagar's endeavor to escape to the cannery lands her in a hospital. In the public ward she again encounters women in a situation similar to her own, but, unlike from Silverthreads, she cannot flee from the hospital and so must reconcile herself somewhat to the strengths other old women collectively offer her. Further, the relative abilities found within the hospital community enable Hagar to offer help when she could have been depicted as most helpless. She finally accepts the strength harbored by community and can accordingly defy her previous overriding superiority and desperate self-containment. Once in the hospital, she laments how little space she has, telling readers, "Lord how the world has shrunk" and "The world is even smaller now. It's shrinking so quickly now" (Laurence 1964, 254, 282). Now that her world is so reduced that she truly is physically contained, she surpasses her previous circumspection and opens herself to friendship with fellow patients. As Michel Fabre puts it in "The Angel and the Living Water: Metaphorical Networks and Structural Opposition in *The Stone Angel*," "[g]radually, through the slow but inevitable ripening of her flesh and her heart, she is led to accept things as they are, to appreciate and accept those elements that she had before considered as scornful, even intolerable, in her own personality" (1996, 27). The need and even desire for others has long plagued Hagar because she has also craved self-sufficiency. She succumbs to what she considers a distasteful weakness of flesh and so becomes able to make interpersonal connections she has also previously considered the result of weakness. Although she never reconciles herself with bodily change to the extent of describing her own body in literal terms, her relations with fellow patients indicate a physical acceptance different from the bathetic metaphors that continue.

Hagar's initial reluctance to share the public hospital ward reflects the disdain she presents herself as having held throughout her life. The "barracks" are "bedlam," and she is forced to sleep "cheek-by-jowl with heaven knows who all" (Laurence 1964, 255). The anonymity of the "mewling nursery of old ladies" gradually dissipates as Hagar listens to them sleep (265): "[S]ome snore raspingly. Some whimper in their sleep. Some neigh a little, with whatever pain or discomfort is their particular portion" (256). She can no longer separate herself from these women when she learns from Elva Jardine and Mrs. Reilly that she too contributed to the nighttime din. Further, when her son Marvin is unable to stay at the hospital, he leaves Hagar in the company of the other patients, whom she witnesses helping each other to attract the nurse's attention. When she discovers that she and Elva Jardine both come from rural Manitoba and even know some people in common, she can accept a connection between herself and the others: "Our eyes meet. There's an amiability about this woman" (272). Her prairie farming connection allows her once again to be called by her proper name, Hagar.

Hagar finally finds strength and acceptance through the other women in the hospital, but both arrive too late for her to contemplate restructuring her world to accommodate communal living. Her story resembles the life review model that is most typical of career selves. Because the only places she encounters women like herself are institutions that forebode ill and limit movement, Hagar only glimpses the possibilities inherent in female friendship and community. Having isolated herself socially earlier in life through her marriage to Bram Shipley and professional relationship with Mr. Oatley, Hagar does not have a basic understanding of the strength of female community to build on in late life. By layering themes (present and retrospective), Laurence underlines Hagar's self-imposed isolation, and she, ironically by her own previous pleading, is finally segregated from the group of women she comes to appreciate.

Nighttime obliterates the connections among the women—"talk between bed and bed is extinguished. Each of us lives in our own night" (273)—but Hagar is able to comfort herself by thinking of the women she has begun to know during the day. When Marvin finally finds the semiprivate room his mother has demanded, her dismay renders her unchanged in his eyes because she still simply seems unhappy with everything he does. He does not comprehend that her desires have changed as the result of newly developed personal relationships. Within the semiprivate room, the change within Hagar that allowed her to appreciate female community in the general ward is reinforced. Hagar is now so intent on making connections that she offends her young roommate by implying that they are similar simply because their fathers share an occupation: "But that's the wrong thing to say. So much distance lies between us, she doesn't want any such similarity" (288). The two are momentarily united when Hagar shares the language of the young woman's generation: "I have to smile at myself. I've never used that word before in my life. *Okay*" (301). Hagar's newfound emotional warmth takes up an extremely small portion of the novel, and it merely suggests a potential, which later works expand, for the portrayal of female-female friendship.

"Brave Again": Joan Barfoot's *Charlotte and Claudia Keeping in Touch*

What Hagar begins to find at the close of *The Stone Angel,* the central characters of Joan Barfoot's *Charlotte and Claudia Keeping in Touch* fully live out in a novel that exceeds the life review model typical of career selves and embraces the possibilities of a seriatim self. The novel charts the developing friendship between two women, now approaching seventy. Their complementarity exceeds their commonality to the extent that they play completely different roles in their separate stories. Charlotte is the other woman in her central romance, and Claudia is the wronged wife in hers. The different stories are narrated alternately, as in *Duet for Three,* so readers have a similar task of aligning and realigning themselves, this time in a friendship rather than a battle. These women look beyond the role each other has played and maintain a crucial intimate bond. They demonstrate that a pairing of women can signify more than merely amorphous femininity eager, or at least willing, to further narratives structured around the goals of male characters. Readers have to rethink affinities continually because they first side with the other woman, then with the wronged wife, and then strangely, somehow, with both.

The support the women continue to offer each other illuminates the strength of complementarity that Gardiner stresses; As Claudia muses, "[p]erhaps between the two of them, Claudia and Charlotte, they've managed to create one single, whole, full life. Maybe Claudia actually relished, the way she could Bradley's body, Charlotte's excursions into what must have looked like wickedness; and maybe Claudia gave Charlotte a relationship, however remote, with solidity and normalcy; at least of the sort promoted by certain kinds of magazines" (Barfoot 1994, 85). The differences between the women allow them to offer something otherwise lacking to each other and to be fulfilled by their interactions. Similarly, readers can imaginatively engage with the completion gained by the constructed experiences of these two elderly characters. Though it is too simple to suggest that they too benefit from the completion, readers might gain a new way of thinking about how female friendships can offer fulfillment.

In describing their friendship, Claudia depicts their separate choices as entailing both loss and gain: "'You don't get to have both, by and large. So you chose interesting, and lost out on ordinary. Me, I chose ordinary, so I couldn't have thrills and change'" (Barfoot 1994, 236). The two overcome what could have easily been, especially from Claudia's perspective, irrevocable differences in a lasting and supportive friendship. Their mutual support extends into a decision to spend their late lives together. In making an unconventional but logical choice, the female characters agree to benefit from close contact with the other side of their crucial earlier choices and, to a degree, gain the "interesting" and "ordinary" they had previously missed. The novel deliberately oversimplifies the dilemma of banality versus excitement to exaggerate how female interactions can help to overcome difference and compensate for loss. More important, the novel depicts these lives moving into a new phase that exceeds the past dependence on a male figure.

Readers witness Claudia, having helped her philandering husband to a swifter end via morphine, write to Charlotte after a year of silence. Charlotte, disturbed by her own recent turn to spying on her former lover from hedges, responds with a warm invitation. The resulting meeting allows the two old women to understand the strength of their collective experience, and they decide to move in together to combat their excruciating memories and perilous financial states. Charlotte expresses the potential of their friendship strengthened into a new living arrangement: "Well. It's only, I thought it would be cheaper for both of us, for one thing. But also it might keep us from driving ourselves crazy. You wouldn't have to be off brooding in that house on your own, and I wouldn't get frightened or tempted by foolishness. I can see getting brave again, instead of ridiculous" (257–58). Instead of continuing to be the wronged wife and the forgotten mistress, the two women can function together socially and combat their fears of late-life fatigue, senility, and decline. Their commonality as older women living changing lives exceeds the complementarity that existed primarily in relation to men.

The friendship these two women have managed to forge becomes more crucial to them than any relationships they have developed with men or even offspring. As Claudia thinks, "Their friendship is a spine that has grown with them, and whatever aches and pains and inflexibilities it has developed here and there, now and then, its absence is not imaginable. What would one be without a spine?" (162). They become mutually dependent to the extent that they share a support system. Neither is entirely dependent, and so neither is vulnerable to outside accusations of insufficiency; instead, they require each other. Claudia has an option other than moving in with her offspring, and Charlotte does not have to move into a nursing home. As a result, when Claudia confesses murder to Charlotte, Charlotte offers comfort, thinking, "Well. Friends perform certain acts, no matter what" (251), and she expresses worry for Claudia rather than for the man Claudia killed.

Charlotte repeatedly says to Claudia in her letters and in person, "'I think we tried to look after each other. I think that's what friends do'" (235). The friendship depicted between these two women hints at a world of possibility for female late life: Neither woman will remain alone in an unsustainable home, neither woman will depend on family to an extent that she may lose the freedom she has finally gained, and neither woman will go to an institution unnecessarily. The two will budget together and explore the numerous possibilities they had been unable to pursue because their opposing love choices interfered with their friendship. As Claudia puts it, "'It's nice anyway, ending up with a friend'" (260).

This fictional exploration of two old women regaining contact to further their friendship at a crisis point in both their lives offers rich insight into the potential for female friendship to offer respite to women at any time, and especially in late life. Never having been able to (or chosen to) make their friendship central in their adult lives, the women realize that doing so could provide a solution to their financial and emotional woes. Readers witness the complex memories and justifications of both women with regard to extremely different experiences and perceive that friendship can offer respite and even escape from the vicissitudes that social hatred of old age can bring. Rather than writing a retreat into lives lived in retrospect, Barfoot depicts the characters as willing to begin anew late in life.

"Ourselves, Up to a Point": Cynthia Scott's *The Company of Strangers*

In *The Company of Strangers,* the characters literally embark on a new journey that is quickly interrupted when their bus lands in a ditch, an accident that could be a simple metaphor for the typical sidelining of elderly women. These characters turn to each other and develop friendships that become the means by which they explore their varied pasts. Career selves meet seriatim selves resulting in a new narrative model, neither entirely fictional nor entirely documentary. Originally called *The Bus,* Cynthia Scott's NFB production is a semidocumentary in which, as actor Mary Meigs puts it in her book-length narrative about the filming, "'our eclectic group of seniors' is being taken in a rented school bus . . . 'to a Golden Age exchange program at some remote resort.' . . . The bus 'runs gently off the road into a ditch,' says Gloria, as we make a detour to find Constance Garneau's childhood house" (1991, 9–10). Cynthia Scott and Gloria Demers chose the group of actors/subjects because of their different backgrounds, but, with the exception of Michelle Sweeney, 27, who drives the bus, the women are all 65 or older: "Alice Diabo, 74; Constance Garneau, 88; Winifred Holden, 76; Cissy Meddings, 76; Mary Meigs, 71; Catherine Roche, 65; Beth Webber, 80" (10). They play themselves, and there is no attempt to hide their particular ages and backgrounds. As a group, they succeed to a larger degree than the characters I have discussed thus far in reshaping devastating understandings of old age, in part by thoroughly investigating the device of the lens as a kaleidoscope for their aging bodies and in part through interdependence.

Meigs talks about the significance of the borders between fiction and nonfiction and between young and old:

> We are ourselves, up to a point; beyond this point is the "semi," a region with boundaries that become more or less imprecise, according to our view of them. In one sense, it is semi from beginning to end, for we wouldn't be out there in the wilds, wouldn't have boarded the bus together. Semi has worked to put together

> seven old women and a younger woman who would never have known of each other's existence, with the ironic outcome that both in real life and on film we become friends who now need to keep in touch with one another. A real documentary might not have had this effect; it might have isolated each of us in her own life and surroundings. (59)

The strength of community is obvious in Meigs's account of the process, but she also discusses how the women individually and collectively grapple with the possibilities that a partially fictional medium affords them. They also wrestle with the disjunction between those possibilities and what they perceive as reality in their own nonfilmic worlds. A documentary "purports to present factual information about the world outside the film" (Bordwell and Thompson 1997, 42), as does *The Company of Strangers.* Further to that standard definition, as John Izod and Richard Kilborn describe John Grierson's innovation, "the documentarist must deploy a whole range of creative skills to fashion the 'fragments of reality' into an artefact that has a specific social impact: that is educationally instructive or, in some measure, culturally enlightening. This account must be, in Grierson's phrase, a 'creative treatment of actuality,' being aesthetically satisfying while also having a clearly defined social purpose" (1998, 427). The NFB's most popular film (according to promotional material) creates a fictive scenario through which to access the seemingly accurate information about old age, gleaned from the women's experiences and conversations. The film works creatively with "fragments of reality" and aims for a social impact that is realized, to some degree, within the film itself.

Writing about women's autobiographical videos, Julia LeSage makes much of "women's fragmented consciousness" (310). She explains, "Unlike social-issues documentarists working over the same twenty years in a realist mode, most of these women artists do not presume to represent a continuous stable identity or a cohesive self. Rather, they pursue an epistemological investigation of what kinds of relations might constitute the self" (1999, 311). *The Company of Strangers* fits to some degree three of the four structures that LeSage articulates as categories of experimental feminist video autobiographies. It collects family photographs, explores daily life, and situates the autobiography within a fiction frame. Writing about the NFB production, Diana George discusses the interactive role of these structures when speaking of the photographs featured onscreen to accompany the oral narratives: "[B]ecause they are so obviously taken from the attics and albums of each actor, the viewer is forced to move back and forth between genres, never settling on the photographs as either evidence or fiction" (1995,

27). The film offers characters, but the characters are at times indistinguishable from the actors. Thus LeSage's fragmented consciousness makes the mix of fiction and documentary appropriate; Catherine Russell describes *The Company of Strangers* in this way: "The fictional premise dislocates the women from their ethnographic characters, and then lets documentary seep in from the edges" (1999, 219).

Meigs provides her own definition of semidocumentary: "A semidocumentary is a happening within an artistic structure, which is set up with a delicate instinct for possibilities, for recognizing the moments at which possibilities happen" (1991, 148). The insertion of fiction into documentary adds the potential of Bakthinian dialogism. In return, *The Company of Strangers* partially thwarts the usual properties of a fiction film because the characters are not mostly imaginary or entirely constructed, but the location and events are. The possibilities available to the fictional aspect of the film uniquely depend upon the participants' link to a lived reality. Meigs tries to explain the thin line between fiction and nonfiction: "We are all 'in real life,' since we are ourselves in a semidocumentary, or 'alternative drama.' Our semi or alternative category shapes our story, which has no plot and no conventional drama; it is a happening in which strangers become company" (9). "The Bus" has the possibilities of narrative, the imaginative detours of fiction, and yet a uniquely permeable boundary between characters and actors. The actors were cast based on their diverse backgrounds, and they are called upon to play themselves, if awkwardly scripted at times. The casting and the effects of the casting amplify changes both to the proposed screen version of the story and to the personal experiences of the actors.

The impact of the film on the participants is uniquely relevant to the film itself. The process of filming results not only in a version that differs from what the directors had envisioned, which is typical, but also in a self-image that differs from what the actors had understood. And it is, in part, that self-image that the film seeks to convey. Meigs explains that "Gloria's scenarios had suggested a 'story,' but this film had been taken by the wayward movements of the cast away from and beyond the 'story' to an unanticipated place where it wanted to live" (29). Thus, the process of creating a fictional narrative of aging had the effect that I propose that reading narratives can have, in that it created a new narrative of aging. The women's emerging friendship revolves around collectivity both in the fictive world they share, where they work together to survive, and in the nonfictive world they share, where they work together to create a narrative.

When Constance complains to Meigs that nothing *happens* in the film, making it a poor example of narrative in her opinion, Meigs responds, "*[W]e* are what happens. The film is about seven semi-old women and a young woman happening" (78). The women themselves are an experience, thwarting conventional understandings both of film and of old women. Old women are not typically viable subjects for a film, so Meigs's response may not go far to alleviate Constance's misgivings. In the process of filming, the women present various concerns about whether they will come across as themselves or as the characters they portray, as old or as semi- old, as their mirror images or as the movie stars dressed up as the old women they frequently refer to themselves as: "ourselves, who were radiant film stars disguised as old women" (38). They fear that the necessary privileging of the visual required by film will limit how they will be seen and how they will be able to see themselves.

Despite their emerging belief in movie illusion, the old women do not entirely overcome a strong belief that their bodies are typically considered inappropriate for display. The problem crystallizes in Meigs's repeated reference to a bathing scene that director Cynthia Scott wanted to film while the actors were naked: "We are asked one by one, how do you feel about walking nude into the lake? That's how I understood the question, though Cynthia tells me that it was hedged with delicate precautions, which, in my panic, I didn't even wait to hear. My horror of the idea must go back to the irreversible prudery instilled in me seventy years ago" (61). Meigs claims that her fear of nakedness comes from internalized notions of appropriateness and the display of female bodies, but the rest of her discussion makes it clear that a fear of exposing old flesh pervades the women who are asked to disrobe. They feared physical ridicule, exposing that their bodies were in fact old: "We were semi-old. It was a lovely illusion that got us through long days without falling in our traces like decrepit cart-horses. It was the reason for our refusal to be in a nude scene, for wouldn't this have proved that we weren't semi but *old*?" (74) Despite some of the women's continued reservations, the directors film a compromise scene. Because of the camaraderie developing among the actors, a clothed scene in the water turns into a childish, teasing water fight:

> "Grotesque, ridiculous, they're trying to make a laughingstock of us," says Constance about our splashing scene; she is looking through the eyes of a hostile audience. But the camera keeps rolling while we (Cissy, Alice and I) become ourselves as little children and, fully clothed, chase each other into the dazzling lake, scooping up warm water as we go. Alice goes in up to her waist, heaves gallons of water at Cissy and me; Cissy and I shriek in mock terror. (61)

Strangely, although the fear of nudity overcame the desire to be made new by the camera and produced a preventative embarrassment, the women did not have the same fear of acting youthful, even childlike. The moment captures to a degree the developing intimacy among a group of old women and helps release the tension in the film's loose narrative about the struggle to survive while stranded in rural Quebec. Still, the tranquility originally envisioned dissipates partly because old women's bodies are not credited, in this case, even by themselves and partly because the directors were unable to come up with an alternative.

Meigs's version of Cynthia Scott's actual vision of the scene is oddly removed from what occurs in the film. Scott tells Meigs she had no intention of fully exposing the women or having them parade naked in front of cameramen. The scene would have been filmed by a woman, and the actors would have worn bathing suits: "The seven of us in the calm lake with our backs turned—that was Cynthia's vision" (74). Her sense of loss in connection with the scene is intensified by an understanding that the actors compensated for remaining clothed by splashing about like children. The potential for the kind of disjunction (between imagined youth and actual age) of posing naked is possibly even more present in the scene as filmed than in the envisioned scene. Somehow it is more appropriate that old women mimic the ridiculous, giddy games of children than that they expose their flesh.

Meigs speaks of the film as "the first time in our lives we are separated from our mirror- images, the ones we can control, and have become Others" (75). She recounts an experience Constance told her about: "She tells me about the stranger riding beside her on a department store escalator, a well-dressed, attractive woman who looked like her and to whom she turned at the ground floor. She felt that she knew her and wanted to greet her. The woman had vanished; she was Constance's mirror-image. Constance realized with surprise that her mirror-image could please her as long as she was a stranger" (76). The women have a similar experience reconciling themselves with their filmic images. Meigs speaks of recognizing herself on the screen after having participated in the illusion of her semi-oldness: "During the entire filming we are invisible to ourselves, but each must have had a private image different from the one we see when we are shown the film. How strange she is, I think of the Mary I see; she has a slow, creaky voice and a face like her mother's crackleware teapot" (78). Meigs wonders about the new realization, whether it lies with the medium or a subjective reevaluation that occurs differently in mirror gazing: "We are seeing our new selves—the real ones? or the ones that others see? It must be this, for the others don't seem strange to us, as each of us is strange to herself" (78). The entire process of creating an illusion has changed Meigs's relation with her physical manifestation so that she no longer feels stuck within the only perspective available from within that physical frame: "Because we are sealed into our bodies, we are surprised by things in ourselves that we have never noticed and that now seem exaggerated and slightly embarrassing" (74). As a result of movie magic, the same process that allows them to turn chicken legs into frog legs during filming allows them to believe in a new physical freedom: "We can bask in a whole summer of attention, we are acting out the myth of our ideal selves, off- and on-camera, and we come to believe in our new reincarnations, there in the centre where the perspective lines meet. It doesn't matter that we, flesh and blood old people are being translated into a film-language that expresses old people (us seven, at least) to Cynthia, Sally, Gloria and others" (77). It does not matter, to Meigs, that an illusion is being created for a semifictive exposé of old age. She and the group of seven women had an opportunity to forge a new relationship with an ideal self not subject to the usual social dicta. The semi of the semidocumentary opened the door for the old women to realize the potential of fiction in recreating their self-images.

The interaction among the women actors is crucial to their capacity to reimagine themselves. As Meigs points out, only by understanding that because she is seeing the others on film as she sees them regularly, she must also see herself as others see her. The filming process brings new ways of seeing from the perspective of each of the women as well as bringing together a diverse group of people who, as Meigs admits, otherwise would not have met. Meigs's description makes clear that the women became friends both on- and off-screen simultaneously: "In the first rushes, Sally says, we seemed (as we were) almost strangers to each other. Our becoming friends off the set changed the nature of the film and made scenes of discord or violence impossible" (77). The kind of community the women form is so strong that it affects the type of film that is made and precludes a previously planned death scene. Originally, Constance's pouring of pills into the lake resulted in her death, but the women grew to know and understand each other so well and developed such faith in the movie magic that they could not actually film that death.

Meigs explains the fictive power of the developing friendship: "The story of the film is the story of the eight pieces of us coming together, an invisible and motionless progress, a gravity pulling toward the still centre that is the place of art" (47). Meigs describes the blending of people into an aesthetic that transforms old bodies for film viewers as part of the developing friendship: "Mixing, not only in terms of sound, but also in the mixture of us: connection or binding, each with every other, and all of us with the elements" (153). The strength of the developing bonds makes even prickly Constance tell Meigs, "'I'm very fond of you. . . . I feel you filled a gap in my life'" (87), and motivates Gloria to ask, in a child's line, "'will you be my friend forever?'" (98). That strength also affects the technical aspects of filming and postproduction. Meigs's figure of speech, mixing, evokes the splicing of the sound track, not the editing of a visual scene, to describe the friendships that emerge as complexly as the film encourages viewers to perceive the women.

The award-winning *Company of Strangers* is of course a selection of the many hours of shooting into a compact narrative with decidedly documentary moments. The conversations among women take the place of talking-head interviews and could make the overall narrative thrust seem contrived, except that the landscape is so carefully woven into each conversation as well as into the overall story (they are stranded within the landscape after all) that the willing suspension of disbelief includes accepting moments of awkward disclosure. The setting operates metaphorically so that the two houses comment on the old age the women face. The building isolated near the water offers a tranquil but lonely refuge. The other decrepit dwelling turns out to be full of hidden treasures that the women, because of their own lengthy experience, understand. The quilt they unearth represents to them hours of careful handiwork. The bizarre and disturbing Victorian bootjack shaped like a woman's body provokes different reactions in the women based on their various relationships to pornography and feminism. The discoveries happen early in their stay and offer an opening to the development of understandings among the women. The metaphors do not veil the aging bodies but rather comment upon them and enhance how viewers can see and interpret them.

The interrupted journey that offers these women the time they share by the lake in rural Quebec can be thought of metaphorically. No longer as able to travel forward, physically hampered from activities previously crucial to everyday life, the women are offered the time and space to discover each others' knowledge, strengths, and stories. Because they do not have food to sustain them, in this extreme case they rely on each others' expertise to survive. Read literally, the film offers the possibility for a group of women to work together, even in late life, to survive a potentially traumatic, life-threatening time. In addition, *The Company of Strangers* shows that constructive bonds can develop out of such interdependence.

Rather than the figures of speech Hagar hides behind, which indicate scorn and contempt for her own changing physical form and the cultural meanings it encompasses, Scott's filmic juxtapositions poignantly link old bodies to surroundings without avoiding the bodies themselves.

Those bodies, the real old women chosen to play themselves, establish friendships that sustain their late lives both in fiction and after filming. Forming interpersonal bonds means finding spaces of interdependence that offer new and continued strengths and experiences. Without evading the visible implications of growing old, the film works through the visual to demonstrate a range of viable tactics for understanding late life, all of which rely on a female community.

Conclusion

The aftermath of the 2000 U.S. election demonstrates how negative assumptions about old people collapse under scrutiny. As it became clear that absolutely nothing was clear about the election results in Florida, blame on old people began. Reporters explained that Palm Beach has a disproportionately large elderly population who must have been confused by the butterfly ballot. For example, a Seattle TV station (K5) focused a human-interest spot on old people to discover whether they would be able discern how to vote for Gore rather than Buchanan. And the elderly became the butt of jokes: A Jay Leno skit depicted an old man with a flowery shirt counting votes very slowly. When Leno talked to him, he got confused and began to count again. As was the case with the (mostly) Canadian ice storm, immediately after the American election, old people's supposed confusion represented what was in fact a much larger phenomenon. That is, it was not only the elderly who could not manage the ballots. A university professor in South Carolina told me of her own troubles with a punch ballot similar to the much-discussed butterfly design. She punched holes in what she thought was the right way, but then she realized that the punches did not hit the perforated holes. She tried to punch again and just caused more random holes. Her request for a second ballot was grudgingly granted, and she was able to make her vote properly (Westphal, personal interview, November 15, 2000). Her experience is no doubt that of many nonelderly, educated Americans who also found the ballot confusing.

The intense irony of the Palm Beach situation came to light days after the furor hit the media. A reportedly distraught supervisor of elections, Theresa LePore, explained that the apparently confusing design occurred because of attempts to take the needs of the elderly into account: "I was trying to make the print bigger so elderly people in Palm Beach County can read it," said LePore (<http://www.salon.com/politics/feature/2000/11/07/results/index.html>). LePore and presumably many others who tested the ballot to ensure its effectiveness chose to focus on one aspect of aging in lieu of another. That is, assumptions about physical infirmity took the place of understanding the experience of these individuals. Undoubtedly the elderly electors have experienced a number of ballots (at least fourteen federal elections have occurred in their lifetime) that consistently and by law ask voters to make an "x" to the right of the name of the candidate they choose. Presenting them with such a ballot yet again would doubtless have been less confusing than the misguided yet presumably well-intentioned attempt to take possible new needs into account.

The automatic blame placing and negative thinking that accompanies media coverage of events such as the ice storm and the American election come directly from negative connotations of the adjective *old.* I seek to alter the interpretive meaning of that adjective in connection with people. Constructive literary and filmic depictions of the elderly offer counterconnotations of *old.* My involvement with fiction and film, centered on late life, challenges how those stages of life resound culturally. I hope that this study continues and encourages many such reinterpretations so that *old* does not have to denote solely incapacity, frailty, decline, death, or dependence.

As I mention briefly in chapter 2, the American translation of Simone de Beauvoir's *La vieillesse* differs in title from the Canadian/British version, even though the rest of the translation is identical. Where Americans encounter *The Coming of Age,* Canadians and Britons find *Old Age.* The euphemistic choice by U.S. distributors fascinates me in its evasion. Implying both a passage into adulthood and a distance, as though people are immune to age until a certain point, *The Coming of Age* appeals to an audience who can remain in denial. Because of my goal to change the interpretive meaning of typical signs of old age, such as wrinkles, institutional care, and continual retrospective narration, I have tried to avoid euphemism in my study. It is my hope along with Barbara Frey Waxman that people will cease to invest in the binary opposition between youth and old age. The two main descriptive terms I choose are *old age* and *late life. Old age* is a blanket term meant to encompass many stages of life. It is discernible only in relation to others, and it is realizable only in a complex engagement with physical and social factors. *Late life* is meant as a relative term. I recognize that *late* might imply an impending mortality, but it also accurately captures where people ages seventy and above, the objects of my study, are located in their progress along Waxman's age continuum. If that implication is problematic, the problem only supports my work as a whole: Progress along an age continuum can be as positive as it is thought to be negative.

I have tried to emphasize, through an interdisciplinary lens, how different modes of talking about age can shift the meaning of *old.* My analysis of the CBC ice storm coverage exposes how, to date, old age represents cultural vulnerability at times when a scapegoat is needed. In *To Live in the Center of the Moment: Literary Autobiographies of Aging,* Waxman explains, "It is an axiom among literary critics and theorists that a reader's response to a text reveals as much about that reader—family background, education, values, life experiences, membership in various communities, personal needs, and the times in which she or he is living—as it does about the text" (1997, 4). Likewise, de Beauvoir claims that the way in which a culture treats old people says more about the culture than it does about old age. Many of the texts I write about are new or concentrate on topics that make critics too uncomfortably self-aware. As a result, much of this narrative fiction has not received serious scholarly attention until now, and what scholarly attention has been directed toward these narratives for the most part fails to satisfy. The diminished attention literary critics pay to age as a category of analysis reveals much about the field. A denial of aging pervades academic disciplines to the extent that even fields that have to work hard to avoid analyzing old age, such as literary studies, manage to evade or denigrate it, as evidenced by the majority of *The Stone Angel* criticism. By analyzing contemporary fiction and film, I hope I have opened up the possibilities inherent within both narrativity and old age. Narrative fiction can encourage a reimagination of social problems, such as ubiquitous negative conceptions of late life. Old age can offer many previously absent boons, such as emotional freedom, intense intergenerational relationships, and the more obvious impressive cumulative knowledge. It is my hope that the adjective *old* can evoke cultural specificity, wonder, awe, excitement, and, most important of all, potential.

I have focused here on social possibilities available to old women at a point when they can no longer manage to live alone. That dilemma forces an evaluation of crucial assumptions about aging, family responsibility, and interpersonal dependence. Where an elderly relative and/or one's aging self should live is possibly the most pressing and widely relevant North American concern with regard to age. I think it also taps into many people's worst fears. The idea that a person may become dependent threatens whatever stability and boundaries one has set up in one's life. The fear that we might be called upon to take in our mother/mother-in-law or place her in an institution pervades our thinking about age. The horror that we might become dependent in other people's eyes to the extent that we may need to live with our offspring or in an institution causes us to defer old age until it is no longer avoidable. For this reason I chose to work from within three choices at that pivotal moment and to unpack the implications of each.

Other focuses would provide especially rich examinations of literary depictions of old age. A study of aging sexuality could be particularly fruitful. A comparative examination of national literatures of aging would comment potently on the cultural specificity of the construction of age. A study with a focus on masculinity and age in fiction and film would complement the work I contribute to here. Explorations of poetic works about aging could amplify both the means of constructing age and the structures that define genre production. An engagement with personal narratives would offer a deep evocation of what it means to live as an old person.

I unquestionably and unapologetically privilege narrative in this study. However, my work will gain strength only in a dialogue with a series of studies in other disciplines. There has to be more than one way to combat not aging but ageism. Though I have been especially critical of medical assumptions and practices throughout, geriatric medical teams as they are conceived in some North American facilities present a model for the type of academic work I think needs to continue on aging. The University of Western Ontario's Western Centre for Continuing Studies' annual conference "Directions in Geriatric Medicine" states that "recognizing the interdisciplinary nature of geriatric care, streams of study are designed for physicians, nurses, therapists, nutritionists, social workers, and discharge planners, as well as people serving in primarily administrative functions" (<http://www.uwo.ca/cstudies/gerimed/>, no longer available). Under the heading "Philosophy," the University of Sherbrooke Geriatric University Institute (Quebec) explains its commitment to interdisciplinary teams: "Interdisciplinarity is defined by a regrouping of many caregivers, each having a specific training, competence and expertise, who work together with the beneficiary, respecting appropriate values in order to arrive at a comprehensive, common and unified understanding of the situation and to a concerted intervention within a complementary sharing of work (<http://www.iugs.ca/missionang.htm>). Interdisciplinary teams prevail in Canadian geriatric medical institutes and serve as a model for gerontological study. The disciplines currently working together within hospitals to care for the elderly, though, do not typically, if ever, include humanities approaches. For genuine, far-reaching benefits of multidisciplinary study, a dialogue among a wider range of disciplines, by no means an easy undertaking, must take place.

Notes

Notes to Preface

1. I am grateful to Barbara Frey Waxman's postulation of a continuum of age to avoid a damaging young/old dichotomy (1990, 8).

2. See Margaret Morganroth Gullette's pivotal essay "Age Studies as Cultural Studies" for an explanation of "age studies" as opposed to "aging studies" (2000b).

3. The impetus to describe old age as comprising stages, in the plural, comes from Erik Erikson, who has elucidated eight stages of psychosocial development that innovatively consider old age to contain development and not merely decline (1964). I suggest that old age can be further differentiated, though it is not the goal of the current study to name stages of psychosocial development.

4. I use the term *fiction* to refer to prose writing on paper and the term *narrative fiction* as a collective term for both film and such prose.

5. The process of growing old and male is distinct from, but related to, the processes I describe here, so that my study has relevance for ongoing cultural analyses of age and gender.

Notes to Introduction

1. The CBC did not save recordings of its ice storm coverage, so I have not been able to obtain a transcript. Some of the radio citations are from my very vivid memories and personal transcriptions of the broadcasts. Because of the emergency circumstances (e.g., working by candlelight), I was not able to keep as accurate a record of the dates and times of the particular quotations as I would have liked, so this analysis encompasses my impressions of a media event. References to "Voices of the Vulnerable" refer to the transcript that the CBC provided to me.

2. I refer here to a longstanding Cartesian tradition of separating mind and body. In *Volatile Bodies: Toward a Corporeal Feminism,* Elizabeth Grosz speaks of three scholarly legacies of that duality: the body regarded as object, the body figured as instrument, and the body as conduit of human expression (1994, 8–9).

3. The rhetoric of "visibility" pervades many identity-based social movements,

and Woodward firmly situates age studies in relation to other academic disciplines with similar goals in articulating a need for greater visibility, citing feminists such as Barbara Macdonald (ix). In her poignant essay, "Look Me in the Eye" (first published in the early 1980s), Barbara Macdonald renders the metaphor devastatingly concrete. She describes a situation wherein her physicality is interpreted as lacking in the context of another movement also seeking visibility for women (a Take Back the Night march); she explains, "this increased visibility of young women is certainly due in part to the efforts of the older women of the first wave" (1991, 37). A march monitor spots Macdonald amid marchers and speaks to her younger lover about Macdonald's capacity to "keep up," suggesting the sixty-five-year-old woman might be better off at the front of the march, reserved for those with difficulty marching. Macdonald, devastated, describes a disturbing process: "It becomes more clear that the present attitude of women in their twenties and thirties has been shaped since childhood by patriarchy to view the older woman as powerless, less important than the fathers and the children, and there to serve them both; and like all who serve, the older woman soon becomes invisible" (40).

4. See Harry Moody (1988).

5. In addition, three recent popular feminist explorations of aging (though again not quite the old age I discuss) emerge directly from feminism's "the personal is the political" credo. As second-wave feminists age, they continue an autobiographical tendency in their writing and choose to write about menopause. In recent publications Gloria Steinem, Germaine Greer, and Betty Friedan have each written about late-life changes for women. Their works generalize from their own experiences and draw on a wide range of cultural data to impel further thinking about older women. But all personal narratives are necessarily delineated by a reliance on experience. Notably, all three well-known feminist writers cite a lack of role models for rethinking old age. As Greer puts it in *The Change,* there are "no signposts to show the way" (1992, 12). In a troubling ageist manual for aging, *Getting Over Getting Older* (the title of which represents old age as a disease or at least an affliction), Letty Pogrebin cites Friedan's and Steinem's calls for "nobility" and "power" in the "elder female" in contrast to her own refusal to "welcome age" (1996, 4).

6. Examples of such postcolonial criticism include Kumkum Sangari, who asks, "What are the modes of access into such nonmimetic fiction for contemporary Euro-American, academic, poststructuralist discourse? In what sense are the openings provided by the fiction itself and in what sense are they constructed by the critical discourse?" (1995, 143). I would elaborate on those questions to ask how younger readers can come to fiction about old age and to explore the degree to which the structure of fiction itself provides the opportunity for constructive depictions of age and the degree to which that constructive aging comes from a particular type of engagement with the texts.

7. In "The Race for Theory," Barbara Christian explores the possibility that theorizing may occur in narrative forms (1988). She writes, "For people of color have always theorized—but in forms quite different from the Western form of abstract logic. And I am quite inclined to say that our theorizing (and I intentionally use the verb rather than the noun) is often in narrative forms, in the stories we create, in riddles and proverbs, in the play with language, because dynamic rather than fixed ideas seem more to our liking" (ibid., 68). I am interested in the process of theorizing that can take place in narrative forms and particularly in the creation of stories of aging as an example of that theorizing.

8. I have selected fiction and film for this study mostly because it is in those literary forms that I have witnessed the largest degree of constructive thinking about old age. A number of Canadian plays, especially in Quebec theater, have begun to take on issues of aging in similarly subversive ways, and dramaturgy is one direction Canadian age studies might take, following Anne Davis Basting's lead in the United States. Opera is another field of study that may yet yield intriguing results when scrutinized with an eye to revising cultural understandings of old age. Another large area I do not touch on here is poetry. Recent work in this area includes a focus on the volumes of late-life creativity that have received considerable critical attention from Anne Wyatt Brown (1993), Carolyn H. Smith (1992), and Kathleen Woodward (1980) and Sylvia Henneberg's as yet unpublished *The Creative Crone: Aging and the Poetry of May Sarton, Gwendolyn Brooks, and Adrienne Rich.*

9. I turn to spectatorship for my study in part because narrative film can have an effect similar to what I claim for novels and in part because I am also speaking of film. Spectatorship offers important commentary on the specularity of film, and, by extension, of novels, but I am also interested in its description of a process of engagement with narrative fiction that includes social and political aspects not just of current spectatorship but also of prospective spectatorship. Mayne herself draws on scholarship of reading, such as Janice Radway's work on romance novels, because she feels it is relevant to film spectatorship. I turn to Mayne's scholarship on cinema to comment upon both spectatorship and reading because, like her, I am interested in the larger social process in which each participates. However, a key difference exists between viewing and reading, in part because each invests in the visual in a decidedly different way (as mentioned in the above earlier discussion of Bakhtin, a key difference for age scholarship is the role of embodiment in film as opposed to written text). In my final chapter, I examine that key difference in connection with an innovative semi-documentary about aging, *The Company of Strangers.*

10. Woodward has profitably examined the relationship between the narratives within psychoanalysis and other cultural narratives in her *Aging and Its Discontents* (1991). Some of the essays she collects in *Figuring Age* delve further into the possibilities and limitations presented by a psychoanalytic approach to this subject (1999). Such work influences my own approach here, and in particular it guides my choice not to focus on or significantly draw from psychoanalytic perspectives. Others who find such work more compelling than I have already made crucial advances in the field of age studies with the help of psychoanalysis, and I think there is room for my own different approach in part because of that work. I also fear the possible drawbacks of psychoanalytic approaches to literature that risk treating characters as people and thereby merely diagnosing literary figures. Rosalie Murphy Baum's essay on Margaret Laurence (1996) risks such a treatment to an effect different from the one I seek here. I want to be able to draw larger conclusions about literary effect than that a work is so "real" that its characters can be treated as subject to psychoanalysis. As Judith Mayne puts it, "However much film theorists may think otherwise, the therapeutic analytic situation is not identical or even analogous to the film analytic one, unless of course one wants to practice the kind of psychoanalyzing of authors or characters that has been discredited for some time" (1993, 59). I hope that my approach, concentrating on the degree to which characters and readers are constructed in terms of age identity, complements existing and current work that fits such age identity into a psychoanalytic framework.

Notes to Chapter 1

1. *Une mort très douce* (*A Very Easy Death*) describes Françoise de Beauvoir's dying of cancer and especially describes Simone de Beauvoir's interactions with her mother during that time. The moving testimony is more about disease than it is about old age; as de Beauvoir explains, "You do not die from being born, nor from having lived, nor from old age. You die from *something*. The knowledge that because of her age my mother's life must soon come to an end did not lessen the horrible surprise: she had sarcoma" (1966, 92). Yet she chooses Dylan Thomas's much-cited villanelle as epigraph (as does Margaret Laurence for *The Stone Angel* [1964]). The memoir contains especially memorable descriptions of her mother's aging and dying body that highlight de Beauvoir's general discomfort with physicality. She writes, "The sight of my mother's nakedness jarred me. No body existed less for me: none existed more. Only this body, suddenly reduced by her capitulation to being a body and nothing more, hardly differed at all from a corpse—a poor defenceless carcass turned and manipulated by professional hands" (18). Elaine Marks comments on this ambivalence toward flesh, "What her writing is up to, and this must be a major source of the critics' malaise, is the affirmation that incontinence, like death, is a great equalizer. 'Jean Paul Sartre' with bed sores and incontinent is not very different from 'Françoise de Beauvoir' with bed sores and incontinent. Between the old man who wets his chair and the old woman who wets her bed, the readers of both sexes who await their turn ('qui attendent leur tour,' wrote Pascal) must read that, at the end, sexual difference fades and that the body that remains is the unrestrained, uncontrolled body of the old woman. It is precisely the body that Western culture and, ironically, Simone de Beauvoir herself have labored assiduously to hide" (1986, 199). Marks pinpoints the critical ambivalence within Simone de Beauvoir's writing about old age. Although she devotes an entire treatise to the subject, she never fully reckons with the aging body.

2. For examples of recent studies that combine disciplines to analyze cultural representations of aging see Woodward (1999), Walker (1999), Basting (1998), Pearsall (1997), Featherstone and Wernick (1995), Wyatt-Brown and Rossen (1993), and Waxman (1990).

3. Anne Wyatt-Brown's "Future of Literary Gerontology" indicates that Margaret Morganroth Gullette has an article in press that praises de Beauvoir for her articulation of the social construction of old age (1993, 44). See Gullette (2000).

4. De Beauvoir stresses that memoir is a suitable venue for late-life creativity, perhaps in part because of her own late-life memoirs.

5. One aspect of de Beauvoir's *Old Age* has received sustained critical attention as evidenced by Marilyn Pearsall's volume of that name (*The Other within Us: Feminist Explorations of Women and Aging* [1997]). Pearsall opens the collection with a reference to looking in the mirror as an old woman, which leads into a brief discussion of how this one point in what she calls the "Coming of Age" derives quite logically from *The Second Sex*. As Pearsall notes, Woodward has also connected de Beauvoir's works in the same way in her "Simone de Beauvoir: Aging and Its Discontents." Waxman draws on this notion in her analyses of Reifungsromane (1990).

6. Along with Robert Dubreuilh (Perron and Dubreuilh are said to satirize Camus and Sartre respectively), Perron had fought in the Resistance. When Dubreuilh sets out to form a rival left party, Perron has to support him to some degree through his editorship of *L'espoir,* but defies him by sticking to what he considers an objective and frank report on Soviet work camps.

7. Featherstone and Hepworth have named the "mask of ageing" wherein the "outer body is seen as misrepresenting and imprisoning the inner self" (1995, 227).

Note to Chapter 2

1. Constance Beresford-Howe's 1973 *Book of Eve* offers another example of a Canadian novel that follows Laurence's model for depicting female familial relationships. In that novel, the only emotional ploy that succeeds with the elderly main character, Eva, is to mention her granddaughter Kim, whose scorn she fears and with whom she feels a unique bond that she has been able to sever with all of the other family members.

Works Cited

Fiction and Films

Alford, Edna. *A Sleep Full of Dreams*. Lantzville, B.C.: Oolichan, 1981.
Antonia's Line. Dir. Marlene Gorris. First Look Pictures, 1995.
Barfoot, Joan. *Charlotte and Claudia Keeping in Touch*. Toronto: Key Porter, 1994.
———. *Duet for Three*. Toronto: MacMillan, 1985.
Beresford-Howe, Constance. *The Book of Eve*. Toronto: MacMillan, 1973.
Company of Strangers, The. Dir. Cynthia Scott with Gloria Demers. National Film Board of Canada, 1990.
de Beauvoir, Simone. *Les belles images*. Trans. Patrick O' Brian. Paris: Gallimard, 1966. London: Fontana, 1969a.
———. *The Mandarins*. Trans. Leonard M. Friedman. 1957. London: Fontana, 1960. Trans. of *Les Mandarins*. Paris: Gallimard, 1954.
———. *A Very Easy Death*. Trans. Patrick O' Brian. 1966. London: Penguin, 1969. Trans of *Une mort très douce*. Paris: Gallimard, 1964.
———. *The Woman Destroyed*. Trans. Patrick O'Brian. Paris: Gallimard, 1967. London: Collins, 1969b. Trans. of *La femme rompue*.
Goto, Hiromi. *Chorus of Mushrooms*. Edmonton: NeWest, 1994.
Laurence, Margaret. *The Stone Angel*. New Canadian Library 37. Toronto: McClelland, 1964.
Mootoo, Shani. *Cereus Blooms at Night*. Vancouver: Press Gang, 1996.
Priory, the Only Home I've Got. Dir. Mark Dolgoy. *Challenge for Change/Société Nouvelle*. National Film Board of Canada, 1978.
Sarton, May. *As We Are Now*. New York: Norton, 1973.
Van Herk, Aritha. *No Fixed Address: An Amorous Journey*. Toronto: McClelland, 1986.
You Are Here. Dirs. Owen Kydd, Jordan Paterson, and Gloria Wong. Videocassette. Vancouver: Simon Fraser, 1998.

Secondary Texts

Abel, Elizabeth. "(E)merging Identities: The Dynamics of Female Friendship in Contemporary Fiction by Women." *Signs: Journal of Women in Culture and Society* 6, no. 3 (1981): 413–35.
———. "Reply to Gardiner." *Signs: Journal of Women in Culture and Society* 6, no. 3 (1981): 442–44.

Achenbaum, W. Andrew. "Foreward: Literature's Value in Gerontological Research." In Bagnell and Soper 1989, xiii–xxi.
———. "Images of Old Age in America, 1790–1970: A Vision and a Re-Vision." In Featherstone and Wernick 1995, 19–28.
Adamowski, T. H. "Death, Old Age, and Femininity: Simone de Beauvoir and the Politics of *La Vieillesse*." *Dalhousie Review* 50 (1970): 394–401.
Aller, Loretta, and Harriet Van Ess Coeling. "Quality of Life from the Long-Term Care Resident's Perspective." In Burggraf and Barry 1996, 17–24.
Arthur, Julietta K. *How to Help Older People: A Guide for You and Your Family.* Philadelphia: Lippincott, 1954.
Bagnell, Prisca von, and Patricia Spencer Soper, eds. *Perceptions of Aging in Literature: A Cross-Cultural Study. Contributions to the Study of Aging* 11. New York: Greenwood, 1989.
Bakhtin, Mikhail. *The Dialogic Imagination.* Ed. Michael Holquist. Trans. Caryl Emerson and Michael Emerson. Austin: University of Texas Press, 1981.
———. "Discourse in the Novel." In Bakhtin 1981, 259–422.
———. "Epic and Novel: Toward a Methodology for the Study of the Novel." In Bakhtin 1981, 3–40.
Bal, Mieke. *Narratology: Introduction to the Theory of Narrative.* 2d ed. Toronto: University of Toronto Press, 1997.
Barthes, Roland. *S/Z.* Trans. Richard Miller. New York: Hill and Wang, 1974.
Basting, Anne Davis. *The Stages of Age: Performing Age in Contemporary American Culture.* Ann Arbor: University of Michigan Press, 1998.
Baum, Rosalie Murphy. "Self-Alienation of the Elderly in Margaret Laurence's Fiction." In Coger 1996, 153–60.
Baxter, John. "*The Stone Angel:* Shakespearian Bearings." *The Provincial Review* 1 (1977): 3–19.
Bell, Alice. "Hagar Shipley's Rage for Life: Narrative Technique in *The Stone Angel.*" In Coger 1996, 51–62.
Bleich, David. *Subjective Criticism.* Baltimore, Md.: Johns Hopkins University Press, 1978.
Bliesmer, Mary, and Pat Earle. "Nursing Home Quality Perceptions." In Burggraf and Barry 1996, 27–36.
Bordwell, David, and Kristin Thompson. *Film Art: An Introduction.* 5th ed. New York: McGraw Hill, 1997.
Buckley, Kathy. *Celebrating Ability.* Performance. Lyman Center for the Performing Arts, New Haven, Conn., October 3, 1998.
Burggraf, Virginia, and Richard Barry. *Gerontological Nursing: Current Practice and Research.* Thorofare, N.J.: Slack, 1996.
Burke, Mary, and Mary Walsh. *Gerontologic Nursing: Wholistic Care of the Older Adult.* 2d ed. St. Louis: Mosby, 1997.
Buss, Helen M. *Mother and Daughter Relationships in the Manawaka Works of Margaret Laurence.* Victoria, British Columbia: University of Victoria Press, 1985.
Butler, Judith. *Bodies That Matter: On the Discursive Limits of Sex.* New York: Routledge, 1993.
Butler, Robert. "Age-ism: Another Form of Bigotry." *Gerontology* 9, no. 4 (1969): 243–46.
Christian, Barbara. "The Race for Theory." *Feminist Theory* 14 (1988): 67–79.
Clément, Catherine. "Peelings of the Real." In Marks 1987, 168–71. Trans. Elaine Marks from *Magazine Littéraire* 145 (1979): 25–27.

Coger, Greta M. K. McCormick, ed. *New Perspectives on Margaret Laurence: Poetic Narrative, Multiculturalism, and Feminism.* Westport, Conn.: Greenwood, 1996.

Cole, Thomas R., Robert Kastenbaum, and Ruth Ray, eds. *Handbook of the Humanities and Aging.* 2d ed. New York: Springer, 2000.

Cole, Thomas R., and Ruth Ray. Introduction. In Cole, Kastenbaum, and Ray 2000, xi–xxii.

Cole, Thomas R., David D. Van Tassel, and Robert Kastenbaum, eds. *Handbook of the Humanities and Aging.* New York: Springer, 1992.

Comeau, Paul. "Hagar in Hell: Margaret Laurence's Fallen Angel." *Canadian Literature* 128 (1991): 11–22.

Corker, Mairian, and Sally French. "Reclaiming Discourse in Disability Studies." In *Disability Discourse.* Ed. Mairian Corker and Sally French. Buckingham: Open University Press, 1999. 1–21.

Coslett, Tess. *Woman to Woman: Female Friendship in Victorian Fiction.* Atlantic Highlands, N.J.: Humanities Press International, 1988.

de Beauvoir, Simone. *The Second Sex.* Trans. and ed. H. M. Parshley. New York: Knopf, 1971. Trans. of *Le deuxième sexe: I. Les faits et les mythes. II. L'expérience vécue.* Paris: Gallimard, 1949.

———. *Old Age.* Trans. Patrick O'Brian. Harmondsworth: Penguin, 1977. Trans. of *La vieillesse.* Paris: Gallimard, 1970.

de Certeau, Michel. "The Unnamable." In *The Practice of Everyday Life.* Trans. Steven Rendall. Berkeley: University of California Press, 1984. 190–98.

Deats, Sarah Munson, and Lagretta Tallent Lenker. Introduction. In *Aging and Identity: A Humanities Perspective.* Ed. Sarah Munson Deats and Lagretta Tallent Lenker. Westport, Conn.: Praeger, 1999. 1–22.

Demetrakopoulos, Stephanie A. "Laurence's Fiction: A Revisioning of Feminine Archetypes." *Canadian Literature* 93 (1982): 43–57.

Dimond, Margaret. "Older Women: Social Policies and Health Care." In Burggraf and Barry 1996, 9–15.

"Directions in Geriatric Medicine." *Western Centre for Continuing Studies.* December 15, 2001. <http://www.uwo.ca/cstudies/gerimed/> (no longer available).

Edelman, Hope. *Mother of My Mother: The Intricate Bond between Generations.* New York: Random House, 1999.

Ehrmann, Jacques. "Simone de Beauvoir and the Related Destinies of Woman and Intellectual." In Marks 1987, 89–94. *Yale French Studies* 27 (1961): 26–32.

Enright, Robert. "Pretty Ribbons." *Border Crossings: A Magazine of the Arts.* January (1991): 25–33.

Erikson, Erik H. *Insight and Responsibility.* New York: Norton, 1964.

Erikson, Erik H., Joan M. Erikson, and Helen Q. Kivnick. *Vital Involvement in Old Age.* New York: Norton, 1986.

Fabre, Michel. "The Angel and the Living Water: Metaphorical Networks and Structural Opposition in *The Stone Angel.*" In Coger 1996, 17–28.

Featherstone, Mike. "Post-Bodies, Aging, and Virtual Reality." In Featherstone and Wernick 1995, 227–44.

Featherstone, Mike, and Mike Hepworth. "Images of Positive Aging: A Case Study of *Retirement Choice* Magazine." In Featherstone and Wernick 1995, 29–47.

Featherstone, Mike, and Andrew Wernick, eds. *Images of Aging: Cultural Representations of Later Life.* London: Routledge, 1995.

———. Introduction. In Featherstone and Wernick 1995, 1–15.

Fiore, Robin N. “Caring for Ourselves: Peer Care in Autonomous Aging.” In Walker 1999, 245–60.

Fish, Stanley. *Is There a Text in This Class? The Authority of Interpretive Communities.* Cambridge: Harvard University Press, 1980.

Forbes, William F., Jennifer A. Jackson, and Arthur S. Kraus. *Institutionalization of the Elderly in Canada.* Toronto: Butterworths, 1987.

Friedan, Betty. *The Fountain of Age.* New York: Simon and Schuster, 1993.

Fullbrook, Kate, and Edward Fullbrook. *Simone de Beauvoir and Jean-Paul Sartre: The Remaking of a Twentieth-Century Legend.* New York: HarperCollins, 1994.

Gardiner, Judith Kegan. “The (US)es of (I)dentity: A Response to Abel on ‘(E)merging Identities.’” *Signs: Journal of Women in Culture and Society* 6, no. 3 (1981): 436–42.

George, Diana. “Semi-Documentary/Semi-Fiction: An Examination of Genre in *Strangers in Good Company.*” *Journal of Film and Video* 46, no. 4 (1995): 24–30.

Greer, Germaine. *The Change: Women, Aging, and Menopause.* New York: Knopf, 1992.

Grosz, Elizabeth. *Volatile Bodies: Toward a Corporeal Feminism.* Bloomington: Indiana University Press, 1994.

Gullette, Margaret Morganroth. *Declining to Decline: Cultural Combat and the Politics of the Midlife.* Charlottesville: University Press of Virginia, 1997.

———. “Age Studies and Gender.” In *Encyclopedia of Feminist Theories.* Ed. Lorraine Code. New York: Routledge, 2000.

———. “Age Studies as Cultural Studies” In Cole, Kastenbaum, and Ray 2000, 214–34.

Hendricks, Jon, and Cynthia A. Leedham. “Making Sense: Interpreting Historical and Cross-Cultural Literature on Aging.” In Bagnell and Soper 1989, 1–16.

Hill, John, and Pamela Church Gibson. *The Oxford Guide to Film Studies.* Oxford University Press, 1998.

Hirsch, Marianne. *The Mother/Daughter Plot: Narrative, Psychoanalysis, Feminism.* Bloomington: Indiana University Press, 1989.

Hirschkop, Ken. “Introduction: Bakhtin and Cultural Theory.” In Hirschkop and Shepherd 1989, 1–38.

Hirschkop, Ken, and David Shepherd, eds. *Bakhtin and Cultural Theory.* Manchester: Manchester University Press, 1989.

Iser, Wolfgang. *The Implied Reader: Patterns of Communication in Prose Fiction from Bunyan to Beckett.* Baltimore, Md.: Johns Hopkins University Press, 1974.

———. *The Act of Reading: A Theory of Aesthetic Response.* Baltimore, Md.: Johns Hopkins University Press, 1978.

Izod, John, and Richard Kilborn. “The Documentary.” In *The Oxford Guide to Film Studies.* Ed. John Hill and Pamela Church Gibson. New York: Oxford University Press, 1998. 426–33.

Kadish, Doris Y. “Simone de Beauvoir’s *Une mort très douce:* Existential and Feminist Perspectives on Old Age.” *The French Review* 62, no. 4 (1989): 631–39.

Kaplan, E. Ann. “Trauma and Aging: Marlene Dietrich, Melanie Klein, and Margueurite Duras.” In Woodward 1999, 171–94.

Kart, Cary S. *The Realities of Aging: An Introduction to Gerontology.* 3d ed. Boston: Allyn and Bacon, 1990.

Katz, Stephen. *Disciplining Old Age: The Formation of Gerontological Knowledge.* Charlottesville: University Press of Virginia, 1996.

Kendall, Eta. Personal interview. October 1998.

King, James. *The Life of Margaret Laurence.* Toronto: Knopf, 1997.

Koster, Patricia. "Hagar 'the Egyptian': Allusions and Illusions in *The Stone Angel.*" *Ariel: A Review of International English Literature* 16, no. 3 (1985): 41–52.

Kydd, Owen. Personal interview. December 28, 1998.

Landau, Gail. "Life and the Nursing Home." *The Globe and Mail.* September 22, 1998: A32.

LeSage, Julia. "Women's Fragmented Consciousness in Feminist Experimental Autobiographical Video." In *Feminism and Documentary.* Ed. Diane Waldman and Janet Walker. Minneapolis: University of Minnesota Press, 1999. 309–37.

Lock, Margaret. *Encounters with Aging: Mythologies of Menopause in Japan and North America.* Berkeley: University of California Press, 1993.

Macdonald, Barbara, with Cynthia Rich. "Look Me in the Eye." In *Look Me in the Eye: Old Women, Aging, and Ageism.* 1983. 2d ed. San Francisco: Spinsters Ink, 1991. 25–42.

Maitland, Sara. "Margaret Laurence's *The Stone Angel.*" *Canadian Woman Studies: Les cahiers de la femme* 8, no. 3 (1987): 43–45.

Marks, Elaine. "Transgressing the (In)cont(in)ent Boundaries: The Body in Decline." *Yale French Studies* 72 (1986): 180–200.

———, ed. *Critical Essays on Simone de Beauvoir.* Boston: G. K. Hall, 1987.

Mayne, Judith. *Cinema and Spectatorship.* London: Routledge, 1993.

Meigs, Mary. *In the Company of Strangers.* Vancouver: Talonbooks, 1991.

Mellencamp, Patricia. "From Anxiety to Equanimity: Crisis and Generational Continuity on TV, at the Movies, in Life, in Death." In Woodward 1999, 310–28.

Miller, Nancy K. "The Marks of Time." In Woodward 1999, 3–19.

Mitchell, David T., and Sharon L. Snyder, eds. *The Body and Physical Difference: Discourses of Disability.* Ann Arbor: University of Michigan Press, 1997.

Moody, Harry. "Toward a Critical Gerontology: The Contribution of the Humanities to Theories of Aging." In *Emergent Theories of Aging.* Ed. James E. Birren and Vern L. Bengston. New York: Springer, 1988. 19–40.

Morson, Gary Saul. "Bakhtin, Genres, and Temporality." In *Critical Essays on Mikhail Bakhtin.* Ed. Caryl Emerson. *Critical Essays on World Literature* series by Twayne, 1999. Ed. Robert Lecker.

Nelson, James Lindemann. "Death's Gender." In Walker 1999, 113–29.

Osachoff, Margaret Gail. "Moral Vision in *The Stone Angel.*" *Studies in Canadian Literature* 4, no. 1 (1979): 139–53.

Patterson, Yolanda Astarita. "Simone de Beauvoir and the Demystification of Motherhood." *Yale French Studies* 72 (1986): 87–105.

Pearsall, Marilyn. *The Other within Us: Feminist Explorations of Women and Aging.* Boulder, Colo.: Westview Press, 1997.

Pogrebin, Letty Cottin. *Getting Over Getting Older: An Intimate Journey.* Boston: Little Brown, 1996.

Porter, James I. Foreword. In Mitchell and Snyder 1997, xiii–xiv.

Potvin, Elizabeth. "A Mystery at the Core of Life: Margaret Laurence and Women's Spirituality." *Canadian Literature* 128 (1991): 25–38

"Promoting the Autonomy of the Elderly." *Sherbrooke Geriatric University Institute.* David Teasdale. March 1999. Accessed February 6, 2003. <http://www.usherb.ca/Iugs/missionang.htm>

Rich, Adrienne. *Of Woman Born: Motherhood as Experience and Institution.* Tenth anniversary edition. New York: Norton, 1986.

Rooke, Constance. "A Feminist Reading of *The Stone Angel.*" *Canadian Literature* 93 (1982): 26–41.

———. "Old Age in Contemporary Fiction: A New Paradigm of Hope." In Cole, Van Tassel, and Kastenbaum 1992, 242–57.

Ruddick, Sara. *Maternal Thinking: Toward a Politics of Peace.* Boston: Beacon, 1995.

Russell, Catherine. "Mourning the Woman's Film: The Dislocated Spectator of *The Company of Strangers.*" In *Gendering the Nation: Canadian Women's Cinema.* Toronto: University of Toronto Press, 1999. 212–24.

Russo, Mary. *The Female Grotesque: Risk, Excess, Modernity.* New York: Routledge, 1995.

———. "Aging and the Scandal of Anachronism." In Woodward 1999, 20–33.

Salon staff. "Some Ballots Illegal, Dems Say." *Salon* November 8, 2000. <http://www.salon.com/politics/feature/2000/11/07/results/index.html>

Sangari, Kumkum. "The Politics of the Possible." In *The Post-Colonial Studies Reader.* Ed. Bill Ashcroft, Gareth Griffiths, and Helen Tiffin. London: Routledge, 1995. 143–47.

Shapiro, Elaine. Personal interview. May 25, 2000.

Shepherd, David. "Bakhtin and the Reader." In Hirschkop and Shepherd 1989, 91–108.

Skinner, B. F., and M. E. Vaughan. *Enjoy Old Age: Living Fully in Your Later Years* (subtitle: *A Program of Self-Management*). New York: Warner, 1983.

Smith, Carolyn H. "Images of Aging in American Poetry, 1925–1985." In Cole, Van Tassel, and Kastenbaum 1992, 217–40.

Sobchack, Vivian. "Scary Women: Cinema, Surgery, and Special Effects." In Woodward 1999, 200–11.

Sontag, Susan. "The Double Standard of Ageing." In *An Ageing Population.* Ed. V. Carver and P. Liddiard. London: Hodder and Stoughton, 1978.

Taylor, Cynthia. "Coming to Terms with the Image of the Mother in *The Stone Angel.*" In Coger 1996, 161–71.

Thomas, Clara. "The Stone Angel." *The Manawaka World of Margaret Laurence.* New Canadian Library 131. Toronto: McClelland, 1976. 60–76.

Thomson, Rosemarie Garland. *Extraordinary Bodies: Figuring Physical Disability in American Culture and Literature.* New York: Columbia University Press, 1997.

Van Herk, Aritha. "Desire in Fiction: De-siring Realism." In *A Frozen Tongue.* Sydney: Dangaroo, 1992. 79–85.

———. "Women Who Made a Difference." In *A Frozen Tongue.* Sydney: Dangaroo, 1992. 236–38.

"Voices of the Vulnerable." *The National Magazine.* Canadian Broadcasting Company, Montreal. January 13, 1998.

Walker, Margaret Urban. "Getting Out of Line: Alternatives to Life as a Career." In Walker 1999, 97–111.

———, ed. *Mother Time: Women, Aging, and Ethics.* Lanham, Md.: Rowman and Littlefield, 1999.

Waxman, Barbara Frey. *From the Hearth to the Open Road: A Feminist Study of Aging in Contemporary Literature. Contributions in Women's Studies* 13. New York: Greenwood, 1990.

———. *To Live in the Center of the Moment: Literary Autobiographies of Aging.* Charlottesville: University Press of Virginia, 1997.

Wendell, Susan. *The Rejected Body*. New York: Routledge, 1996.

———. "Old Women Out of Control: Some Thoughts on Aging, Ethics, and Psychosomatic Medicine." In Walker 1999, 133–49.

Westphal, Sarah. Personal interview, May 14, 1998.

———. Personal interview, November 15, 2000.

Woodward, Kathleen. *At Last, the Real Distinguished Thing: The Late Poems of Eliot, Pound, Stevens, and Williams*. Columbus: Ohio State University Press, 1980.

———. *Aging and Its Discontents: Freud and Other Fictions*. Bloomington: Indiana University Press, 1991.

———. Introduction. In Woodward 1999, ix–xxix.

———. "Inventing Generational Models: Psychoanalysis, Feminism, Literature." In Woodward 1999, 149–68.

———, ed. *Figuring Age: Women, Bodies, Generations*. Bloomington: Indiana University Press, 1999.

Wyatt-Brown, Anne M. "Introduction: Aging, Gender, and Creativity." In Wyatt-Brown and Rossen 1993, 1–15.

———. "The Future of Literary Gerontology." In Cole, Kastenbaum, and Ray 2000, 41–61.

Wyatt-Brown, Anne M., and Janice Rossen. *Aging and Gender in Literature: Studies in Creativity*. Charlottesville: University Press of Virginia, 1993.

Zerilli, Linda M. G. "A Process without a Subject: Simone de Beauvoir and Julia Kristeva on Maternity." *Signs: Journal of Women in Culture and Society* 18, no. 1 (1992): 111–35.

Index